A CHARMING EXCHANGE

25 Jewelry Projects to Create & Share

Kelly Snelling & Ruth Rae

NORTH LIGHT BOOKS
CINCINNATI, OHIO
www.mycraftivity.com

My soul wants to fly away
My soul wants to take flight
God said to the mind, "Return from where you came
Your knowledge has brought the question.
And your grace has given the answer.
~ Rumi

WWW.FWPUBLICATIONS.COM

12 11 10 09 08 5 4 3 2 1

DISTRIBUTED IN CANADA BY FRASER DIRECT
100 Armstrong Avenue
Georgetown, ON, Canada L7G 5S4
Tel: (905) 877-4411

DISTRIBUTED IN THE U.K. & EUROPE BY DAVID & CHARLES
Brunel House, Newton Abbot, Devon, TQ12 4PU, England
Tel: (+44) 1626 323200, Fax: (+44) 1626 323319
E-mail: postmaster@davidandcharles.co.uk

DISTRIBUTED IN AUSTRALIA BY CAPRICORN LINK
P.O. Box 704, S. Windsor, NSW 2756 Australia
Tel: (02) 4577-3555

LIBRARY OF CONGRESS CATALOGING-IN-PUBLICATION DATA
Snelling, Kelly and Rae, Ruth.
  A charming exchange. / author. -- 1st ed.
    p. cm.
  Includes index.
  ISBN-13: 978-1-60061-051-6 (alk. paper)
  1. Jewelry making. I. Title.
  TT000.G00 2008
  000.00--dc00
                                   0000000000

EDITOR: **Tonia Davenport**
COVER DESIGNER: **Marissa Bowers**
INTERIOR DESIGNER: **Jennifer Hoffman**
PRODUCTION COORDINATOR: **Greg Nock**
PHOTO STYLIST: **Jan Nickum**
PHOTOGRAPHERS: **Tim Grondin, Al Parrish & Christine Polomsky**

METRIC CONVERSION CHART		
to convert	to	multiply by
Inches	Centimeters	2.54
Centimeters	Inches	0.4
Feet	Centimeters	30.5
Centimeters	Feet	0.03
Yards	Meters	0.9
Meters	Yards	1.1
Sq. Inches	Sq. Centimeters	6.45
Sq. Centimeters	Sq. Inches	0.16
Sq. Feet	Sq. Meters	0.09
Sq. Meters	Sq. Feet	10.8
Sq. Yards	Sq. Meters	0.8
Sq. Meters	Sq. Yards	1.2
Pounds	Kilograms	0.45
Kilograms	Pounds	2.2
Ounces	Grams	28.3
Grams	Ounces	0.035

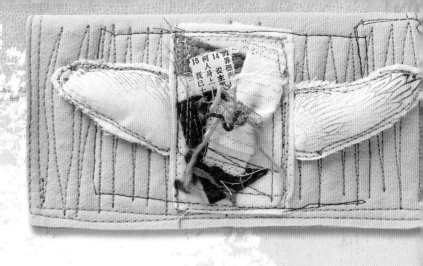

Dedications

For Tom, Finnigan
& Morgan,
**who give my life
constant joy.**

—*Kelly*

To *my amazing family,*
thank you all for supporting
**my crazy, compulsive nature
to create for days** & **weeks at a time!**
Thank you for allowing me
the space in which I need
to grow & **express myself.**
Without your love, I would be lost!

—*Ruth*

Acknowledgments

We would like to thank the fabulous group of artists who participated in this collaboration with us. Thank you for your talents, trust, inspiration and friendship. Thank you to our amazing editor, Tonia Davenport, and the wonderfully creative staff at North Light. We so appreciate your excellent guidance and keen organizational abilities. You all made this entire endeavor much easier and oh-so-much more fun. Lastly, we would like to thank our families for their constant support, encouragement and willingness to let us be crazy jewelry-making women at all hours without our homes falling down around us.

Contents

CREATE & COLLABORATE 62

We will surely get
to our destination
if we join hands.

—Aung San Suu Kyi

Magic Among Members

It is late: The children are finally asleep, the dog has stopped his click, click, clicking behind you, and now you are alone. You can think. This is when the magic starts bubbling.

The art we create is an expression of who we are and how we see the world. Seeds of inspiration can come from one thousand things in an average day: flowers in the garden, a sunset, the evening news or even silence. An artist's gift is to miraculously conjure something from nothing, to turn a dream into a piece of art. Most artists do this all alone.

With the growing number of online art groups, a cloistered regimen doesn't have to be the only way. Even if you live in a tiny town devoid of an artist community, you have the entire world at your fingertips to collaborate with you.

Different from a typical how-to jewelry book, this book contains projects that were collaborations between a group of women, from several countries, of varying skills and talents—artists from many different mediums. You can make the projects in this book by yourself and create lovely pieces. But you can also learn to find inspiration by working with other artists to produce collaborative pieces that can take you down a completely new and exciting artistic path.

That is how this book was born. We all collided on the way to the grocery store of artistic inspiration. It was the summer of 2006. Ruth and I were strangers who had recently joined an online professional artists' group.

Among this group were frequent, collaborative projects and exchanges between the members. Ruth decided to host her first exchange with a charm swap. I had never made any real sort of jewelry before, but when I saw the artists who were signing up to participate, I couldn't stand to miss out on the experience.

When Ruth began this first exchange, she had no idea just how much her mind would be opened. Her background is in metalsmithing, and she had always kept her jewelry work separate from her mixed-media art. By hosting the charm swap she discovered that she could bring the two disciplines together.

Because we were a group of fiber artists, painters, collage artists and mixed-media artists, the resulting charms were created from a variety of nontraditional materials. My charms were made from an iridescent beetle wing and a photo of my grandmother's eyes. Sally Turlington made her charms from an empty nicotine cessation vial previously used in her husband's attempts to quit smoking. Our bracelet even contained minuscule Christmas tree light bulbs, tiny corks, flattened bottle caps and metal from a candy tin. Nothing was off limits with this bunch.

Ruth then created an online blog with photos and step-by-step instructions for each of the twenty-five charms (*www.justsimplycharming.blogspot.com*). The site was an enormous success. Other charm exchanges began to spring up around our online art community.

We thought our project would make a great book, so here it is. We collaborated equally on its contents, though you'll notice the writing is in my voice. We hope that this book is one from which you can easily learn and be deeply inspired. Throughout these pages are many tried-and-true techniques as well as mesmerizing projects. We want this book to ignite your creative energy and inspire you to new heights of artistic expression—alone of in collaboration with others. So come join us in *A Charming Exchange*.

—*Kelly*

Making Jewelry
{BASIC TOOLS & SUPPLIES}

Most of the projects in this book can be made with a few fairly inexpensive tools. We chose to make pieces that used cold connections so that you do not have to solder or use large, menacing equipment. On these two pages are the tools and supplies that you will want to have on hand to make the various jewelry components in this book.

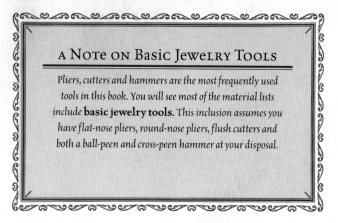

A Note on Basic Jewelry Tools

Pliers, cutters and hammers are the most frequently used tools in this book. You will see most of the material lists include **basic jewelry tools***. This inclusion assumes you have flat-nose pliers, round-nose pliers, flush cutters and both a ball-peen and cross-peen hammer at your disposal.*

Flat-nose pliers: Used to hold and grip wire, these have a smooth, flat edge at the jaw tips. They can be used to make a sharp bend in wire and are also used for opening and closing jump rings.

Chain-nose pliers: Much like flat-nose pliers, these come to a sharp point at the tips and are great for close detail work.

Round-nose pliers: These pliers have tapered, cone-shaped jaws. They are used for making small jump rings, loops and spirals. An extra-long pair can be helpful for making larger loops and curving wire for clasps.

Flush cutters: These provide a nice, straight cut on wire and are used at the start and end of most jewelry components.

Ball-peen (or chasing) hammer: This is our all-around, most-used hammer to flatten and smooth wire. Ruth uses

the 4-ounce size. It is a good idea to use a scrap of felt over the face of your hammer to keep it from becoming marred as you work with it. Dents and other marks on the hammer can transfer to your wire or sheet. The ball side can be used to texture your wire and sheet metal.

Cross-peen (or riveting) hammer: This hammer can be used to set rivets. The long side of the head can be used for spreading metal as well as for creating a cross-shaped pattern or long lines in your metal.

Rawhide or plastic mallet: Use this when work must not be marred. This is used to flatten out sheet metal and for links that need to be flattened or reshaped.

Steel bench block: This is a surface used in partnership with a hammer for adding texture, flattening, straightening and hardening wire and sheet metal.

V-slot board & clamp (bench pin): A support for filing and sawing, it attaches to the edge of your table with a clamp.

Jeweler's saw & saw blades: This saw is primarily used to cut shapes and windows from metal sheet, but once you own one, you may find numerous other uses for it as well, such as cutting apart a coil to create jump rings. A size 2/0 blade works great for 20-24-gauge metal.

A few tips for using this saw: Use beeswax as a lubricant by passing it once over your blade before you start sawing. If you are frequently breaking blades, it's possible that your blade is not secured tightly enough.

Using smooth up and down movements, turn corners by sawing in place as you turn the metal and the frame. Use your fingers to support your work as you saw, keeping it over the open V section of the V-slot board (or bench pin).

Files: We use a 6" (15cm) long, half-round, Swiss-made, medium-grit (2) file. It is a good size for filing a straight edge and a curved edge on sheet metal. You can find this file at most jewelry supply stores or online suppliers. Use your file with your V-slot board and clamp for the best leverage. Remember to file only in one direction.

Mandrels: These are used to wrap your wire around to form a spring of coils that can be cut to make jump rings. They can also be used to help you form large links. With mandrels and your drill you can quickly produce long coils. Wooden dowels and knitting needles (useful mandrel alternatives!) can be found in most craft stores. Piano wire (used to make small coils) can be found in most hobby shops.

Dapping block & punches: This is a cube of metal with circular depressions used with a matching dap and a hammer to create domed metal cups. Dapping tools are punches with a ball-shaped end. This is a great tool to use in conjunction with the disk cutter.

Two-hole metal punch: This is a steel screw-style hand punch that cuts $3/32$" (2mm) or $1/16$" (2mm) holes in silver, copper, plastic or any soft metal up to 14-gauge. It is great for making eyelet holes. You can get one online from companies like Rio Grande, Dick Blick or J.S. Ritter.

Disk cutter: This steel tool is used to cut disks out of soft sheet metal such as silver, copper or brass up to 18-gauge. It is used with a hammer or hydraulic press to drive punches through a ring, cleanly cutting out the desired-sized disk. When used with the dapping block, you are on your way to creating your own domed beads!

Awl: This can be used to make pilot holes in soft metals and wood before drilling or before hammering in rivets or tacks. It is also good for making holes in clay.

Center punch: Use this to mark your spot before drilling to prevent the drill from slipping when you start.

Metal alphabet stamp set: This set of metal stamps is used with a hammer to imprint words into metal.

Electric drill: Besides being used to make holes, a drill is used to twist wire, for jump rings or coils, with the help of dowels or other mandrels.

Ruler: Measure twice, cut once.

Black permanent marker: Use this to mark your cut lines on wire once they have been measured. Also use it to mark your pliers so you can use the same spot over and over when you are trying to make identical links or loops.

Wire: We recommend starting out your jewelry-making experience using brass or copper wire. Both are readily available, easy to work with and inexpensive. We also use steel wire for a few of the pieces in this book. Once you are confident of your skills, you will be ready to move on to sterling silver and gold or gold-filled wire. Wire also comes in different shapes, such as square, half-round and round. We use round the most often.

Wire is measured in gauge; the most common sizes are 14, 16, 18, 20, 22, 24 and 26. The larger the number, the smaller the diameter of the wire. Larger gauges (24 and 26) are good for making bead segments with pearls and small beads, which usually have smaller holes. Twenty gauge is a good size for ear wires and most other projects; it isn't too flimsy but is easy to bend. When making clasps and jump rings, choose a strong gauge. Your choice will also depend on how much weight your jump rings will need to bear.

Beads: Beads have an alluring quality to them. For me they are completely addictive. I am always on the hunt for the perfect bead. Ruth has been making jewelry many, many years, so she has quite a stockpile of every gemstone, bone and pearl, faceted or smooth, in an enormous variety of shapes. There have been times I have suffered bead envy while admiring her collection. So be aware that once you start buying amethysts, garnets and aquamarines, you may discover that you can do without a new dishwasher so you can hoard more beads.

Liver of sulphur: This solution is used for darkening silver and copper. The fumes are strong, so it should be used with good ventilation. We prefer the dry variety (which you mix with hot water) as it seems to stay fresh longer than the liquid does. When reusing your stored solution, it is also helpful to heat under hot water the piece that you want to antique.

Wet/dry sandpaper: Available in three grits (600, 1200, 2000), it comes in sheets that can be cut into four smaller pieces. Start out working with 600 grit and work your way up to 2000 for a finished look on your sheet metal. It can also be rubbed over the top of a piece that has been dipped in liver of sulphur to bring back some of the sheen.

Collaborate or Swap?

{BOTH ARE FUN!}

Collaborating

Most of the artists in this book met one another online. We were members of various creative groups and formed friendships through our art. There are literally thousands of online groups just waiting for people to join them—a different organization for every sort of artistic endeavor. You'd be surprised by how much you can learn, free of charge, right in your own home.

If you would like to participate in an artistic collaboration or swap, a good place to start is with an online forum like Yahoo! Groups (http://groups.yahoo.com). There you will find different groups based on an assortment of common interests, such as artistic media and geographical location, as well as various skill levels. These individuals participate in an ongoing exchange of ideas, techniques and resources. It is a fabulous way to meet like-minded people who will help you jump-start your creativity.

If you don't see a group that speaks to you right off the bat, start your own. You can easily set up a Yahoo! group tailored to your own tastes. Invite people you know to join or leave it open to the general public. Make your own rules and run the group however you envision it. Don't be afraid to dream big.

Another lively way to begin a collaborative exchange is to enlist members of your own family. A charm exchange can quickly turn into the highlight of your annual family reunion. One summer, my mom organized a charm exchange between several female family members to coincide with my yearly visit. Each person made a charm no longer than 1½" (4cm) for every participant. We met at the local library to exchange the charms in person. Each cousin, aunt and sister individually took the floor to show off her creation, explain her inspiration and tell how the piece was made. The next part of the afternoon was spent making bracelets to hang the charms on or adding the charms to pre-made chain. A few of the girls had never made jewelry before, but you certainly wouldn't have guessed that. All the charms were very clever and reflected each participant's personality. I will always treasure the bracelet I created that day.

Also, check out your local bead stores, art supply stores and art guilds. Most of these places not only offer workshops and resources for artists but also may include other artists who are interested in collaboration. Ask if they have a local artists' group that meets regularly, and, if they don't, offer to start one. You can bring in this book and work through the projects with the other artists that you meet. Or you can design your own necklaces, using some of the techniques that you learn here.

Swapping

If you decide to try hosting your own charm exchange, consider the following tips.

For your first exchange, it is wise to start with a small group. Three to five people is a great number to start out with. But even a one-on-one collaboration or swap will prove to be fun. Just remember that communication is the key.

Decide if you want to open your exchange solely to friends and family or to post it online and take all comers. An online exchange is a great way to meet new people all over the world, many of whom may have a refreshingly new perspective on art. Understand up front, however, that there is a risk that someone may back out or send in work that may not meet your expectations. It doesn't always happen, but it can. Be prepared for how you want to deal with such a circumstance.

Select a theme, color palette and metal tone for the jewelry findings. Some folks don't mind a combination of copper, brass and silver, all on one piece, but, if you prefer a more cohesive look, state it up front. Decide whether or not you want everyone to include jump rings with the finished charms. And, if the final piece is a bracelet, it is wise to limit the size of the charms to 1½" (4cm) so you can comfortably wear them all together.

If your participants are not all local to you, charms should be carefully packaged and mailed to you along with funds and a self-addressed label for return shipping. The same packaging can be reused, or extra money should be included for the return packages. If you are dealing with artists from different countries, you will need to include proper custom forms with their packages. Also, be sure to find out if certain countries have any restrictions on what can be sent there. Some do not allow certain types of bone, seeds, feathers and other natural materials to come into the country.

Another excellent way to collaborate and exchange artwork is through a round robin. In a jewelry round robin, each artist begins the construction of a piece. This can be as simple as making chain and a focal piece or simply creating a pendant. After the initial construction, the pieces are sent to each of the artists to work on individually and add their own special elements. Eventually, the piece will go through the entire group, coming full circle back to the originator for a truly collaborative piece of art.

Many artists have started their own blogs showcasing their work and telling their stories. Several people run exchanges from their blogs. If there is a particular artist whose work you admire, you can contact her about collaborating on a piece or about the possibility of an exchange. It is a wonderful way to grow and learn as an artist.

Art swaps and collaborations are an exciting opportunity to see others' art up close and to gain inspiration. We all have strengths and weaknesses, and when we view another person's work and add our ideas to it, the creativity is endless. Watching the evolution of each piece is a thrill like no other. So get busy and start creating!

Here is a list of places to help you get started along your collaborative path.

A Charming Exchange

www.acharmingexchange.blogspot.com
A blog for this book where you can ask questions and talk to the authors.

Art-E-Zine

www.art-e-zine.co.uk
A wonderful site out of the UK with swaps, online workshops, articles, resource lists and inspiring galleries.

Charmed Designs

http://groups.yahoo.com/group/charmed_designs
They swap out smaller numbers of good-quality, handmade art charms, paying close attention to the creative process.

Charms 2007 Swap

http://groups.yahoo.com/group/charms2007swap
They swap larger numbers of great-quality, handmade artistic charms. This is open to advanced artists who work neatly and carefully.

EBSQ Self-Representing Artists

www.ebsqart.com
An online community for the self-representing artist.

Jewelry Arts Lapidary Journal

http://groups.yahoo.com/group/jewelryarts
An online group for readers of Lapidary Journal magazine.

MMCA

www.mixedmediacollageartists.com
An online art group for professional mixed-media, collage and assemblage artists. This is the group where Ruth and I met.

Meet Up

www.meetup.com
A place to connect with other artists sharing similar interests and living in the same area.

Wet Canvas!

www.wetcanvas.com
The Internet's largest online community for visual artists.

Wire-Wrap Jewelry Artists Group

http://groups.yahoo.com/group/wire_wrap_jewelry
An online group that focuses on many types of jewelry.

Yahoo! Groups

http://groups.yahoo.com
A search for jewelry artists at Yahoo Groups' homepage resulted in more than three thousand groups. Surely there is one just right for you!

CONNECT

This section features the results of three different creative endeavors: A collaborative round robin between five artists (who are anything but average), followed by two imaginatively themed swaps that were slightly primitive (talismans and found-object necklaces).

Each of these exchanges will arouse your curiosity and get you thinking outside the box when it comes to elements for your jewelry creations.

We'll begin with a project that will provide you with the perfect housing for these creations, when you wish to present them as a gift, and then we will jump right in with the collaborative works. Throughout this section you will be introduced to ways of incorporating a variety of nontraditional elements into your traditional jewelry-making techniques. In addition, we will continue to discuss the creative stimulus that comes with collaboration.

Collaborating on an artistic project is a fabulous way to boost your skills, discover new inspiration for direction and propel your imagination. It's also outrageously fun. Connecting with other artists naturally enriches our lives. It teaches us a great deal about ourselves and our ability to give freely to others. It is so satisfying to brainstorm design concepts with a group of friends or a mentor. The rapport and confidence that grow from this process elevates the entire experience.

> **The creative person**
> is both more primitive
> *& more cultivated,*
> **more destructive,**
> a lot madder & a lot saner,
> *than the average person.*
>
> —Frank Barron

Jewelry Gift Folder

Ruth Rae

My soul wants to fly away
My soul wants to take flight
to the mind, "Return from where you came"
God said to the mind, "Return from where you came"
Your knowledge has brought the question.
And your grace has given the answer.
— Rumi

MATERIALS

scissors

sewing machine

rubber stamps

felt

quilting thread

cheesecloth

tulle

book text

muslin or other fabric scrap

vinyl

ribbon scraps

StazOn ink pads

Ruth is not only an exciting jewelry artist but also a talented fabric artist. For her, presentation is an essential component of the creative process. A winning example of this is her jewelry presentation folder. She always creates a lovely textile home, for each piece of jewelry, that she gives as a gift.

Ruth loves to get lost in the small details of her fabric pieces. She adds layer upon layer of jewels and treasures within netting, dyed cheesecloth, vintage lace and felt. She joyfully enshrouds them, creating little secrets for the lucky recipient to discover.

She swears these are a snap to make, even for someone like me who turns thread into knots just glancing at a sewing machine. The fun part is that you can add as much or as little to them as you like in the way of details and embellishments. This wrap not only heightens the beauty of the gift but becomes a part of the gift as well. Just imagine the expressions of happiness on your friends' faces when you present them with gifts that are so exquisitely wrapped.

Folder for Bracelet

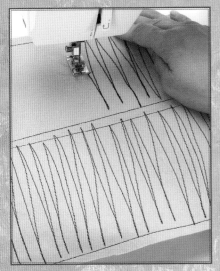

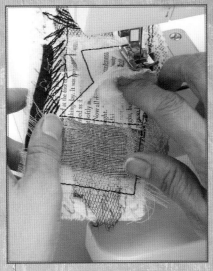

{1} ADD STITCHING TO FELT

Cut a piece of felt to 9" × 9" (23cm ×23cm). Fold it in half to crease it, then unfold. Using a sewing machine threaded with quilting thread, sew a straight stitch around the perimeter of the piece and along both sides of the fold. Then sew a free-form zigzag stitch across the width of both halves.

{2} SEW TOGETHER LAYERS

From this point it is a layering process, and it's really up to you how you want to embellish your folder. Here, I have made a stack of several layered things: a stamped piece of fabric, a piece of felt, some cheesecloth, some tulle, a piece of torn book text and, finally, a pocket of fabric with a stamped phrase. Sew all the layers together at once. Sew around the small pocket piece, leaving one side open to fill with a small amount of batting.

{3} ADD LAYERS TO FELT

When you're done sewing the layers together, sew the piece to the front of the folder.

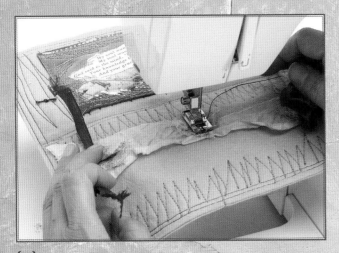

{4} ADD A STRIP OF FABRIC FOR JEWELRY

You can repeat a similar process for the inside of the cover. I sewed a layer of vinyl over my layers. To create a place for the jewelry, sew a scrap of fabric (such as muslin) to the back, layered over two small strips of ribbon on either end.

{5} SECURE JEWELRY INTO FOLDER

Lastly, tie the jewelry onto the ribbons to finish.

For this collaboration, five first-class artists, Ruth Rae, Jessica Moreau-Berry, Deryn Mentock, Crystal Neubauer and Catherine Witherell, each created a themed necklace or bracelet, using a limited number of elements. Each piece was rotated through the mail from one artist to the next, each adding her own mark to the piece while celebrating the intent of the original creator.

GOTHIC ROMANCE

ORIGINATOR: CATHERINE WITHERELL
CONTRIBUTORS: RUTH RAE, DERYN MENTOCK, JESSICA MOREAU-BERRY & CRYSTAL NEUBAUER

MATERIALS

14-gauge wire

18-gauge wire

20-gauge wire

24-gauge wire

½" (13mm) dowel

³⁄₁₆" (5mm) dowel

basic jewelry tools (see page 8)

wool roving

liquid dish soap

vinegar

felting needle

file

charm

Catherine Witherell was the originator of Gothic Romance. Her plan was to make a chain of medium-sized sterling links (plain and twisted wire) that were doubled and used no solder. As a centerpiece, she created a red felted heart. Catherine then sent her creation on to Ruth.

When Ruth saw Catherine's necklace she immediately knew she wanted to add some chain mail to it. She imagined a broken heart that had been stitched up. So, she domed a piece of copper sheet to create a heart and "stitched" it up with wire. She then added chain mail with a few beads to create Brave Heart, Ruth's addition to Catherine's stunning necklace.

As the work progressed, all the artists posted images of their additions to the group's website. The excitement this created was palpable. They were able to discuss the process as it was happening even though everyone lived far apart. All were open to sharing information about the techniques that were used, supplies, design strategies and more. The entire process really stirred up the artistic passions of all the participants, and it surely shows in the final product.

Double-Ring Chain

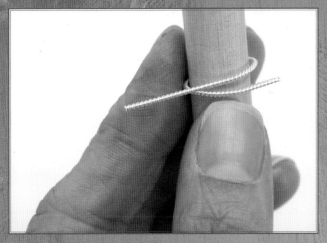

{1} SHAPE WIRE AROUND DOWEL

Twist enough 24-gauge wire to create twenty-nine 3" (8cm) pieces. (See page 109 for instruction on twisting wire.) Also cut twenty-nine 3" (8cm) pieces of 20-gauge wire. Using a ½" (13mm) dowel, wrap each piece around the dowel, overlapping the ends.

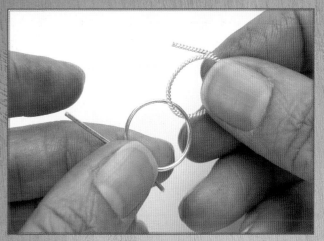

{2} ALTERNATE LINKS

Connect one plain wire link with one twisted-wire link.

{3} WRAP TO SECURE

Wrap the ends around each ring to secure them together.

{4} CONNECT RING PAIRS

Repeat steps 2 and 3 to create twenty-nine connected rings. Create fifty-four jump rings from 18-gauge wire using a ³⁄₁₆" (5mm) dowel. (See *Missing Link*, page 113, for instruction on creating basic jump rings.) To assemble the chain, connect each pair of rings with two jump rings.

MISSING LINK

The collaborative process becomes a delicate balance of knowing when to create something new for the piece and when to merely embellish what is already there. A collaborative project is a fantastic opportunity to see the handiwork of talented artists up close and to be inspired by it.

Felted-Heart Charm

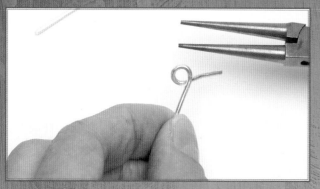

{1} CREATE A LOOP
Cut two pieces of 14-gauge wire to 1⅞" (5cm). Create a loop in the center of one piece.

{2} LINK TWO WIRE PIECES TOGETHER
Create a loop in the second piece and link the two together. Lightly sand the ends of each piece with a file.

{3} SHAPE HEART
Wrap the roving around the armature to form and shape a heart.

{4} FELT ROVING AND RINSE
Felt the heart by rubbing it with your fingers in a bowl of soapy water. Squeeze and continue to rub the shape, keeping the bottom nice and pointy. Continue for about five minutes. You'll feel the heart shape shrink and harden slightly. Rinse the heart in vinegar. Give it a more refined shape by using a felting needle.

{5} SHAPE WITH NEEDLE
Leave the heart to dry overnight. Add any final shaping with the needle if needed.

{6} CREATE WIRE WRAP FOR HEART
Cut a 6" (15cm) piece of 20-gauge wire and make an eye at one end, with the excess wrapped around the base of the loop. Push the wire through the heart from the top to the bottom and create another eye loop at the bottom.

{7} SECURE JUMP RINGS AND CHARM
Add two jump rings to the eye at the top and one to the eye at the bottom. The top jump rings will attach the heart to the necklace and the bottom can hold a charm.

To say this round robin stretched me as an artist would be putting it mildly! I learned so much through this experience. I learned techniques in wire wrapping and assembly that I hadn't previously known. I learned to look at other artists' work and adapt my style to theirs. I learned to overcome many fears and insecurities about my abilities and to trust myself and let go.

It was a real challenge to begin my necklace and not complete it. It was difficult to have a picture in my mind of what it should look like and not to include every element I imagined for it. I had to force myself to stop working on it. I wound up sending it off with a letter pointing out things the other artists could do to complete it. But, in the end, each artist was so true to her own style and did things I never would have imagined. The necklace turned out even more wonderful than I had pictured! I discovered the freedom of letting go and enjoyed the process of it unfolding.

I felt so incredibly blessed to be included in this group of talented artists and to be able to collaborate with them on this project. I wouldn't trade this experience for the world, and I was sad to see it come to an end. But I do feel I have made friendships through the process that will continue, and who knows—Round Robin II, anyone?

—Crystal

History Lesson
{OBJECT AS ART}
Crystal Neubauer

Contributors: *Ruth Rae, Catherine Witherell, Deryn Mentock & Jessica Moreau-Berry*

Forest Fairy

ORIGINATOR: JESSICA MOREAU-BERRY
CONTRIBUTORS: DERYN MENTOCK, CRYSTAL NEUBAUER,
RUTH RAE & CATHERINE WITHERELL

Round Robin

MATERIALS

18-gauge wire

20-gauge wire

26-gauge wire

½" (13mm) dowel

basic jewelry tools (see page 8)

steel bench block

faceted glass, 2 pieces

image

black polymer clay

gold-leaf kit

assorted beads (4mm—8mm)

size-14/0 seed beads

For Jess Berry, jewelry involves "junque"—a fancy word for vintage treasures. Jess's inspiration for her Forest Fairy piece came in a couple of unique ways. She took her first wire jewelry class the day before she made her necklace. She had a blast in the class and came up with these fabulously original and funky links for her necklace. When it came time to design her pendant, she did what any clever artist would do and made the best of a bad situation. She had been revamping her studio and stepped right onto a lovely vintage tray. Jess was devastated

for about twenty seconds until she realized the glass would make an awesome pendant. But if you don't want to smash your vintage treasures, look for a stained-glass supply store in your area or online. In the example that follows, in which I made a similar pendant, I used some faceted glass squares that were originally intended for a stained-glass window. You could also use microscope slides, large glass bubbles or, with the right tools, glass from old bottles.

Gilded-Clay Pendant

{1} SANDWICH IMAGE
Sandwich a collage between two pieces of glass. (Here, I'm using two pieces of faceted glass from a stained-glass store.)

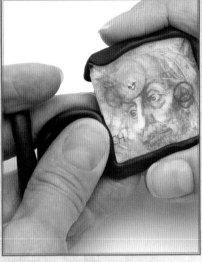

{2} WRAP GLASS IN CLAY
Condition some polymer clay and roll it out into a thin snake. Press the clay around the perimeter of the glass sandwich, and press it slightly on the front and back edges of the glass to ensure that it will hold the glass in.

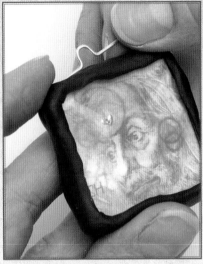

{3} ADD WIRE BAIL
Cut a length of 20-gauge wire to about 1½" (4cm). Bend a U shape in the center and press it into the top of the clay for a bale.

{4} APPLY LEAF ADHESIVE
Bake the piece according to the clay manufacturer's directions. Brush gold-leaf adhesive onto the clay.

{5} ADHERE GOLD-LEAF PIECES
Let the piece sit for the recommended amount of time (until it becomes tacky), and then apply small amounts of gold leaf. Rather than covering the entire surface, I let some of the clay show through for a distressed look.

{6} SEAL THE LEAF
Seal the leaf with the manufacturer's sealer.

Decorative Links

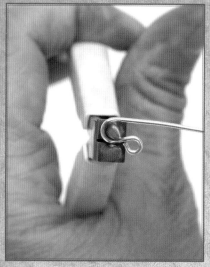  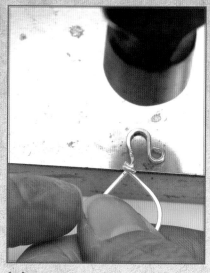

{1} MAKE A SMALL LOOP

To make a few decorative links, cut 4" (10cm) of 18-gauge wire and make a small loop at one end. Then bend the wire in the opposite direction to start to create a large tear-drop shape.

{2} COMPLETE WRAP AROUND DOWEL

Mold the wire around a ½" (13mm) dowel, and then wrap the wire around the base of the small loop at the top.

{3} HAMMER LINK

Hammer the hook portion and the round portion, but be careful not to hammer the wrap. Repeat for as many links as you like.

Wired Web & Spider

 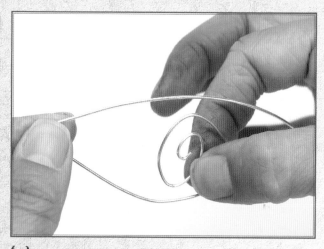

{1} BEGIN SHAPING LEAF

Cut an 11" (28cm) length of 18-gauge wire. To form a leaf for the spiderweb, at about 5" (13cm) from the end, bend the wire to create a point for the leaf.

{2} COIL THE INSIDE

Coil one end into a free-form spiral.

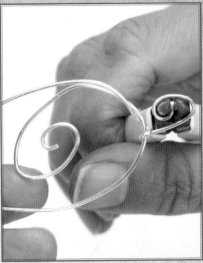
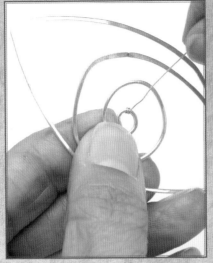
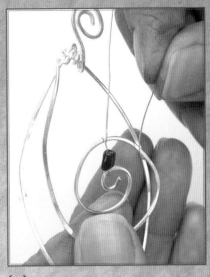

{3} SECURE SHAPE WITH WIRE

Join the two sides of the leaf by wrapping the other end of the wire around the coil a couple of times, and then coil the remaining wire in the opposite direction as the larger coil.

{4} ATTACH WIRE TO COIL

Lightly hammer the entire piece. Cut a long length of 26-gauge wire and connect it to the inside of the larger coil.

{5} ADD A BEAD

Thread on a bead, and then wrap the wire on the other side of the spiral.

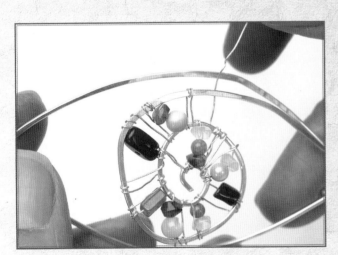
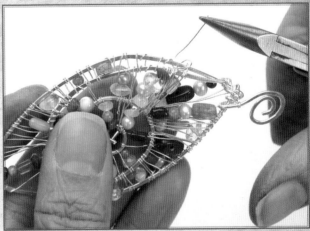

{6} CONTINUE BEADING AND WRAPPING

Continue adding beads and wrapping wire, following the direction of the coil.

{7} SECURE WIRE WHEN LEAF IS FULL

Continue adding beads and wire until the spiral is full. Wrap the excess wire around the top to secure.

{8} WRAP AROUND SEED BEADS

Cut a 4" (10cm) length of 26-gauge wire and thread two size 8 and two size 4 seed beads onto it for the eyes. Make a loop with the beads in it, and wrap the wire around the base.

{9} WRAP WIRE FOR BODY

Trim the excess from the wrapped tail. Thread on a 6mm bead, then an 8mm bead, and then wrap the wire between the two.

{10} ADD WIRE FOR LEGS

Cut three 5" (13cm) pieces of 26-gauge wire. Wrap the three as a group around the body-head connection.

{11} THREAD BEADS AND MAKE LOOPS

Thread fourteen size-14/0 seed beads onto each leg. To hold the beads onto the wires, make a tiny loop at the end of the beads, using pliers.

{12} SECURE SPIDER TO LEAF

Position the spider where you want it on the web and thread the wires through. Secure the leg wires to the spiral wire by wrapping each around the web a couple of times.

Usual Suspects
{UNUSUAL & UNIQUE ELEMENTS}

Deryn Mentock

Contributors: *Ruth Rae, Catherine Witherell, Crystal Neubauer & Jessica Moreau-Berry*

Deryn Mentock started off the unusual-elements aspect of her chosen theme by adding a charm made of a silver dental crown with a pearl embedded in it—surprisingly uncommon but exceedingly lovely. Here, she gives her take on this collaborative experience:

"I have to admit that I went into this project with a little apprehension, as I didn't know most of the participants very well. However, this added an element of excitement, too. Each time I received a piece of jewelry, it was like a revelation of the owner's personality and of those who had already contributed to the piece. Holding the jewelry in my hands and examining it up close, I had more than one ah-ha! moment. The whole project has been so creatively stimulating—much more so than I would have thought. All these things and seeing everyone put a little bit of her soul into each piece have been very touching and created a connection with this group that I will remember every time I look at my own lovely necklace from the project.

"I think the thing I take away most is that connection. I loved working collaboratively with like minds, loved seeing what the artists before me had done and figuring out how to complement that. As the pieces passed from artist to artist, I could see the progression from a basic piece of jewelry to something stunning and unique. Thank you all for a wonderful experience!"

Little-Wing Souls in Flight

ORIGINATOR: RUTH RAE
CONTRIBUTORS: DERYN MENTOCK, JESSICA MOREAU-BERRY,
CRYSTAL NEUBAUER & CATHERINE WITHERELL

Round Robin

MATERIALS

1mm × 4mm rectangular wire

16-gauge wire

18-gauge wire

24-gauge metal sheet

8mm dowel or mandrel

basic jewelry tools (see page 8)

steel bench block

jeweler's saw

drill and size 28 bit

vise

center punch

file

fine-point permanent marker

small piece of Plexiglas

image

Ruth is a true romantic at heart. In her fabric art she creates splendidly layered pieces with mysteriously hidden jewels and whispered secrets buried in every fold and lace-draped pocket. Her bracelet in this round robin is no exception. It is an exotic, dream-drenched sentiment for the wrist with many shrouded wishes. One of Ruth's favorite quotes is from the French author André Gide, who said, "Art is a collaboration between God and the artist, and the less the artist does, the better." Surely she must have done very little here, because her winged bracelet is heavenly.

Ruth created her centerpiece for the bracelet using sheet metal, Plexiglas, resin-coated religious texts and rivets. The entire bracelet is a beautiful example of her excellent metalsmithing skills. The richly textured links create a gorgeous backdrop for the alluring additions of the other four artists.

Bar/Loop Links

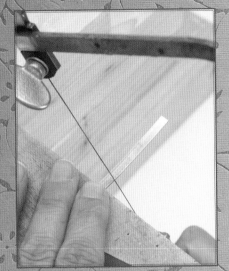

{1} TRIM RECTANGULAR WIRE
Cut six lengths of 1mm × 4mm wire to 1½"
(4cm), using a saw or heavy-duty cutters.

{2} SPLAY ENDS WITH HAMMER
File the ends of each piece. Using a cross-peen
hammer, flatten each piece a bit and splay the
ends. Start in the center, and work your way
out to the ends to spread the metal.

{3} ROLL ENDS INWARD
Using round-nose pliers, roll in the ends
of each piece.

Bar/Loop Clasp

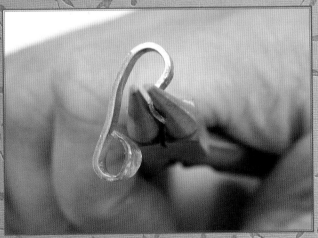

{1} ROLL BAR INTO HOOK SHAPE
To make a hook for a clasp, repeat the process shown above in step 2,
beginning with a 1⅞" (5cm) piece of silver bar, and roll in one end.
For the other end, roll it in a bit, and then roll it in the opposite
direction at the end.

{2} CONNECT LINKS WITH JUMP RINGS
Using an 8mm mandrel, create eight twisted-wire jump rings from
18-gauge twisted wire (see page 112). Connect the rolled links and clasp
with the jump rings.

Plexi-Sandwich Charm

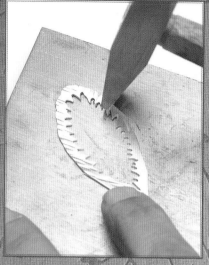

{1} CUT AND PREPARE FRAME

To create a Plexi-sandwich, start by cutting out an oval shape from a 24-gauge piece of silver sheet metal, using a jeweler's saw. Use a fine-point permanent marker to draw a jagged frame shape around the perimeter. Drill a hole somewhere in the center and disengage your saw blade to put it through the hole. Then cut along the lines to remove the opening from the frame portion. Add texture to the frame using a cross-peen hammer.

{2} FILE WIRE ENDS

To create two temporary rivets, trim a couple of pieces of 16-gauge wire to about 3" (8cm). File one end of each piece to make them perfectly flat.

{3} MARK END WITH CENTER PUNCH

Put the flattened end of the wire into a vise and use a center punch to create a dimple in the center of the flat portion.

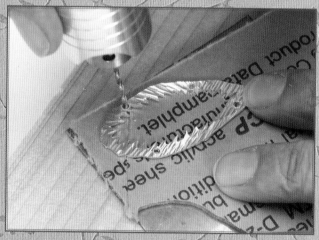

{4} TAP WIRE END TO SPLAY OUT

With a riveting hammer, tap around the perimeter of the wire to splay it out and create a rivet.

{5} DRILL HOLES THROUGH THREE LAYERS

Repeat steps 3 and 4 for the other wire and set the pieces aside. Set the frame on top of a piece of Plexiglas and a piece of 24-gauge metal sheet and drill a hole through all three layers at each end. Avoid positioning your holes too close to the edge, or the frame might crack.

{6} INSERT TEMPORARY RIVETS TO SECURE

Insert the temporary rivets through the holes and bend the wire over in the back to hold everything together.

{7} SAW AROUND SHAPE

Use the jeweler's saw to trim the Plexiglas and copper sheet to the same shape as the frame.

{8} INSERT IMAGE AND RELAYER PIECES

When the piece is cut out, smooth the edges of the entire piece well with a file. Remove the temporary rivets and, keeping in mind how the sandwich will go back together, remove the protective backing from the Plexiglas and trim your desired image to size. Sandwich the image under the Plexiglas and assemble the pieces back together.

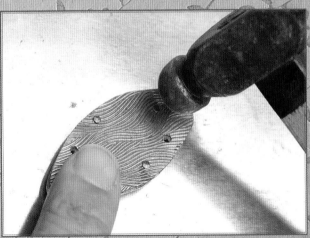

{9} SECURE SANDWICH WITH FINISHING RIVETS

In the same fashion as the temporary rivets (steps 2–4), create rivets for the holes of the piece. Finish the rivets on both sides. (I also gave some texture to the back with a cross-peen hammer.)

The talisman project was set up as a trade. As participants (Deryn Mentock, Martha Brown, Kelly Snelling, Sally Turlington, Cece Grimes, Crystal Neubauer, Lorraine George, Ruth Rae and Catherine Witherell), we were to make a completed piece of jewelry to symbolize a talisman or amulet that would be traded at the end of the project. Each artist was also to include a story about her piece to explain its meaning and intent.

THE SHEPHERD'S AMULET

DERYN MENTOCK

MATERIALS

19-gauge steel wire

22-gauge steel wire

basic jewelry tools (see page 8)

steel bench block

sandpaper

rock, approximately 1½" (4cm)

8mm beads

laser photocopy of image

watercolor crayons

cup of water

paintbrush

gel medium

decorative paper

coin purse or small wallet

The Shepherd's Amulet Bag was Deryn's project and was inspired by one of her favorite passages in the Bible: John 10, verses 27–28, the story of the Good Shepherd and His flock.

The amulet bag itself is a very old leather coin purse she embellished by adding a transfer of Jesus holding a lamb. Many elements added to the purse held symbolic meaning to Deryn. A tourmaline stone with a vintage brass cross represents the Shepherd's sacrifice; a piece of petrified wood, dug from the Shoshone riverbank between Cody, Wyoming, and Yellowstone—two of her favorite places—represents a staff;

a heart-shaped stone given to her by her youngest son represents the heart the Shepherd has for His flock; and hammered links made with green garnets represent the green fields the flocks pasture in. Inside the bag is the Shepherd's guidebook, consisting of pages from John.

Deryn says that although she doesn't believe in the power of objects, this amulet necklace reminds her where the real power in her life lies.

Wrapped-Stone Link

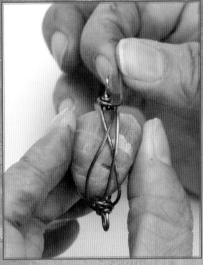

{1} BRING WIRE AROUND ROCK
For a rock link, cut about 16" (41cm) length of 19-gauge steel wire and polish it with sandpaper. Make an eye on one end, leaving a 6" (15cm) tail. Position the rock at the base of the eye and bring the wire around it.

{2} CREATE SECOND EYE
Wrap one wire around the other on the opposite side of the rock, and then create a wrapped eye.

{3} CONTINUE WRAPPING ROCK
Trim the shorter tail. Securely wrap the longer wire around the rock a few more times, wrapping it around each eye as you pass it. Wrap a final time around one eye and trim the wire.

Three-Bead Decorative Link

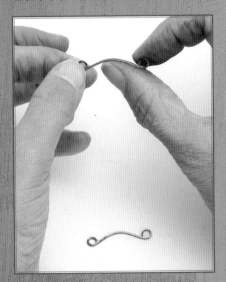

{1} SHAPE LINK HALVES
Trim two 2" (5cm) pieces of 19-gauge steel wire and polish it with sandpaper. Curl the ends inward, and then arc each piece slightly.

{2} HAMMER HALVES
Hammer each piece on a steel bench block to flatten it.

{3} HOOK HALVES TOGETHER
Cut a 3" (8cm) length of 22-gauge wire and polish it with sandpaper. Bend a ⅛" (3mm) hook on one end and, holding the two hammered pieces together, hook it onto one of the pieces.

{4} SQUEEZE HOOK TO SECURE
Wrap the wire around to secure the pieces together and squeeze the hook part flat. Then pull the long end through the other loop, bring it around and squeeze the whole thing again to flatten it.

{5} ATTACH A NEW WIRE
Trim the excess, and then repeat steps 3 and 4 for the other side. Trim a piece of 22-gauge wire to about 6" (15cm) and wrap one end of it perpendicularly around one of the staples from the last step.

{6} ADD BEADS
Thread on three 8mm beads, and then wrap the wire in the same manner around the other end and trim the excess.

Image-Transfer Wallet

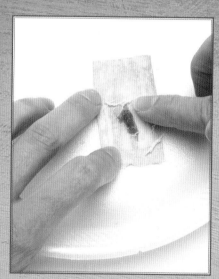

{1} ADD COLOR TO PHOTOCOPY
Create a laser photocopy and color it a bit with watercolor crayons and water.

{2} ADD COATS OF GEL MEDIUM
Apply three coats of gel medium to the piece, letting it dry between coats.

{3} DAMPEN PAPER AND RUB OFF
Brush water onto the back of the transfer and let it sit for a minute. Then gently rub the paper off to reveal the gel-medium transfer. Be patient and don't rub too hard. Do this several times to remove all the paper.

{4} APPLY WET BRUSH TO PAPER
Use a wet brush to trace the general shape of your wallet onto a piece of decorative paper, such as this sheet music.

{5} ADHERE PAPER TO WALLET
Then, where the paper is wet, gently tear it down to size. Brush gel medium over the surface of the wallet where the paper will go, and apply the paper. Brush more medium over the top of the paper.

{6} SEAL TRANSFER OVER WALLET
Apply your transfer over the top of the decorative paper, and then add a final bit of gel medium over the transfer to seal it.

{7} ATTACH WALLET TO CHAIN
Secrure your desired chain (a pre-made chain, or one you created yourself) to the wallet by using a basic wire wrap to attach the chain to the wallet's hardware, such as a keychain, or sew a jump ring to the edge of the leather.

MISSING LINK

A talisman is a lucky charm. Traditionally, the possessor believes it imbues him with something extra, some tiny magic mojo sprinkles on this cereal called life.

EYE OF GOD

LORRAINE GEORGE, RUTH RAE & KELLY SNELLING

MATERIALS

18-gauge steel wire	dimensional adhesive
20-gauge steel wire	(Diamond Glaze)
22-gauge artistic	polymer clay (white,
wire	beige & yellow)
24-gauge artistic	8mm beads
wire	2 beads of your choice
basic jewelry tools	mica
(see page 8)	photo images
craft knife	clipped book text
awl	burnt umber glaze
scissors	permanent marker
1/8" (3mm) hole	metallic paint pen
punch	black acyrlic paint
rubber stamp	assorted colors
eyelet setter	of acrylic paint
1/8" (3mm) eyelets	paintbrush
	(optional)

This talisman is a collaborative piece between three artists. Ruth had asked the talented Lorraine George if she had any additional pieces she wanted to send along for the book. Lorraine sent in a beautiful faux bone polymer clay pendant with an iconic image from a stamp by artist Beckah Krahula. Ruth and I both thought it was absolutely beautiful.

Ruth lives about forty-five minutes away from me. As I drove home from her house, I kept thinking about the pendant. It had captured my imagination, and I couldn't get it out of my mind. I wanted to make some charms to accompany it and lend themselves to the overall feeling of the piece. All the way home I daydreamed about what I would make.

As soon as I got home, I sat down in my studio and made several mica charms to complement the Madonna pendant. I gave these to Ruth, who, in turn, pulled all the elements together with a herringbone wire wrap that we like to call the Eye of God. Perhaps you made something similar with yarn and wooden sticks as a child in summer camp or vacation Bible school. This sophisticated version will work well on many jewelry pieces and will perhaps sweetly remind you of your childhood, as well.

Eye-of-God Link

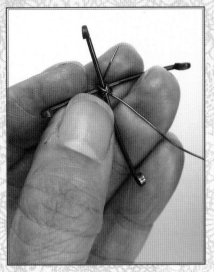

{1} CREATE AN "X"

Cut two 2" (5cm) pieces of 18-gauge steel wire and hammer the ends of both pieces. Curl the ends of both pieces inward. Make an "X" with the wire, and secure it in the center with another "X" in 24-gauge wire.

{2} BEGIN WRAPPING WIRE

Begin wrapping the wire around each of the four posts, going in the same direction for each one. Complete about three rows.

{3} COMPLETE WIRE WRAPPING

Continue around, but wrap the wire in the opposite direction around each post. Wrap until you reach the ends of the posts. Wrap the wire around the final post a couple additional times to secure, and trim the excess.

Bead-Wrapped Link

{1} WRAP ONE BEAD

Cut a 4" (10cm) length of 22-gauge artistic wire and, leaving a 1" (3cm) tail, make a rosary wrap (see page 110 for instruction), wrapping the wire five times. Thread on an 8mm bead, and repeat the wire wrap on the opposite side of the bead, leaving the same amount on each side. (Note: I use the nose of my pliers to measure the length of the first wrap and then to know where to bend the wire for the loop after the second wrap.

{2} SECURE 24–GAUGE WIRE TO BASE BY BEAD

Repeat step 1 to make a total of seven. Then cut a 24" (61cm) piece of 24-gauge wire and wrap the end around the base next to the bead.

{3} WRAP WIRE AROUND BEAD

Bring the wire down the side of the bead, under and around the wrapped arm of the eye pin at the base.

{4} CONTINUE WRAPPING WIRE AROUND BEAD

Continue wrapping the wire in the same direction, always bringing it first under and then around the arm of the eye pin and laying the 24-gauge wire in the channels between the 22-gauge wire on the original wrap, for a total of five wraps around.

Mica-Tile Links

{1} TRIM MICA TO IMAGE

To create mica tile pieces, start by trimming to size the image or text that you want to sandwich between the mica. Then use the image as a guide to trim the mica to the same size. (Note: Mica sheets come in thick pieces that can be split apart into many more thin sheets. You want a sheet that is fairly thin but still strong enough not to split when you set an eyelet into it.)

{2} COLOR EDGE OF IMAGE

Before creating your sandwich, color the edges of the paper using a pen, paint or glaze.

{3} SECURE PIECES

Apply a drop of Diamond Glaze to one side of the image and press on a piece of mica. Repeat for the other side to make your sandwich.

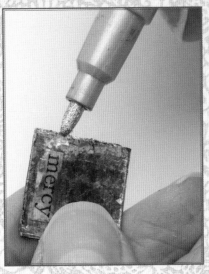

{4} OUTLINE EDGES IN BLACK

Use a permanent marker to outline the edges of the tile.

{5} OUTLINE EDGES IN GOLD

Repeat with a metallic paint pen. (This part is very fun because the paint oozes into all of the mica's fine cracks.).

{6} SET EYELETS

Punch a hole in each side and set an eyelet in each hole. Use the holes to attach the piece to jump rings or other links on your necklace.

Clay Bone Pendant

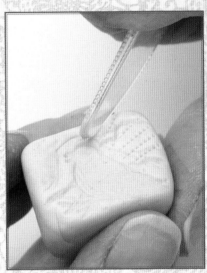

{1} MIX CLAY COLORS

To create the clay pendant, start by mixing equal parts of white and beige polymer clay with a small bit of yellow. The final color should resemble bone.

{2} STAMP INTO CLAY

After the clay is conditioned and mixed, shape it into a block. Stamp into the surface of one side with a rubber stamp.

{3} ADD FINAL DETAILS

Add additional details with a craft knife or scratch awl.

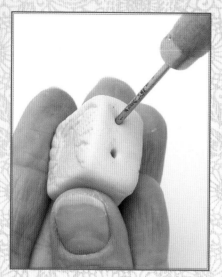

{4} MAKE TWO HOLES

Make a couple of holes through the piece using an awl.

{5} APPLY PAINT AND GLAZE

Bake the piece according to the manufacturer's directions. Rub thinned black paint over the piece, and then wipe off the excess with a paper towel. Repeat using burnt umber glaze.

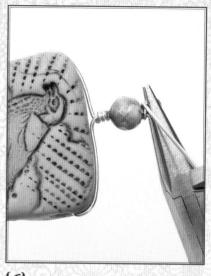

{6} ADD WIRE AND BEAD

Thread a 5" (13cm) piece of 20-gauge wire through the top two holes and wrap one piece around the other. Thread a bead over both pieces. Then create a loop at the top with a second wire wrap.

{7} HAMMER LOOP

Hammer the loop of the wrap.

{8} ADD SECOND BEAD

Repeat for the bottom, adding a rosary-wrapped bead (see page 110 for instruction).

{9} APPLY COLOR TO IMAGE

If you like, you can paint the completed piece with acrylic paints.

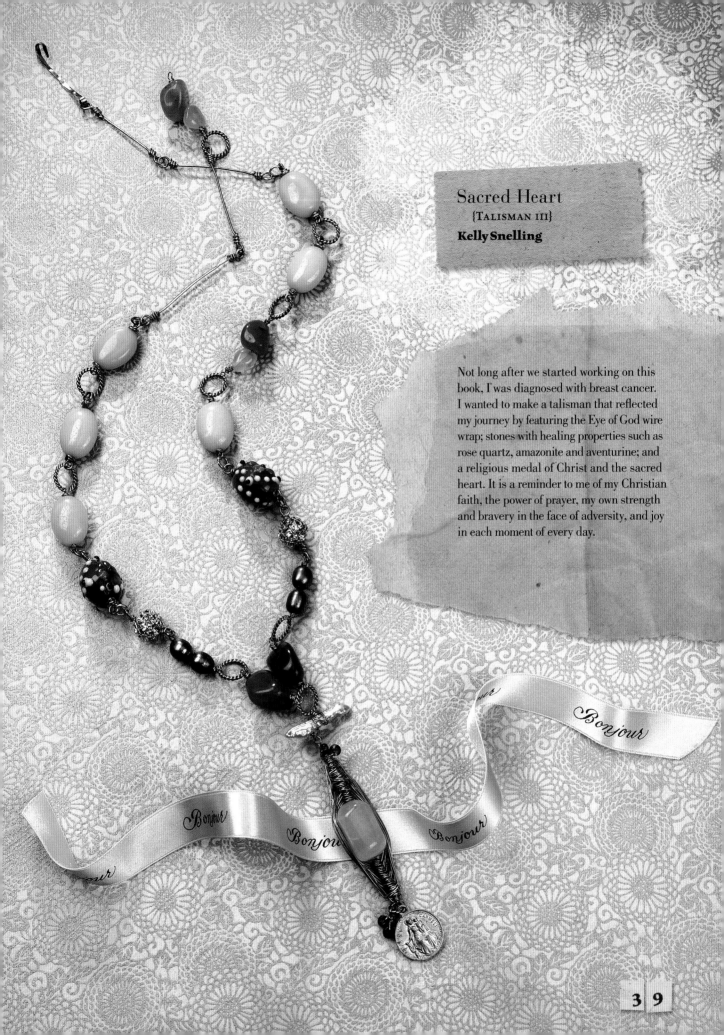

Sacred Heart
{TALISMAN III}
Kelly Snelling

Not long after we started working on this book, I was diagnosed with breast cancer. I wanted to make a talisman that reflected my journey by featuring the Eye of God wire wrap; stones with healing properties such as rose quartz, amazonite and aventurine; and a religious medal of Christ and the sacred heart. It is a reminder to me of my Christian faith, the power of prayer, my own strength and bravery in the face of adversity, and joy in each moment of every day.

My Healing Mandala was created "all in fun." It is an object of art straight from my imagination. It contains colorful herbs, flowers and barks such as snakeweed, cornflower and rose hips—with healing properties—all surrounding a "guardian angel."

—*Sally*

Healing Mandala
{TALISMAN IV}
Sally Turlington

Protection
{TALISMAN V}
Catherine Witherell

This talisman is for the pocket. It is the symbol for death. On one side are the words *singing* and *I love you, you, you* trailing down. It protects the love of the one who holds it, and the love for the one who wears it, until the death of one of these people or the loss of the amulet. The other side has three patterns almost seamlessly changing into each other, signifying that the love of those involved will be constant throughout all the changes that their life together will bring.

—*Catherine*

the Origin of Strength

CRYSTAL NEUBAUER

Talisman Swap

MATERIALS

18-gauge wire

20-gauge wire

24-gauge wire

basic jewelry tools (see page 8)

drill

liver of sulphur

vinegar

charm

Crystal Neubauer created her talisman with a gorgeous wire basket centerpiece. She ingeniously made the small basket by weaving steel wire and suspending an old mother-of-pearl cross, taken from a rosary, inside it. Crystal's talisman is based on verse 2 of Corinthians 4:7, "But we have this treasure in jars of clay to show that this all-surpassing power is from God and not from us."

Crystal explained it like this: "In the Bible, the term 'jars of clay' represents our human frailties. The treasure inside the jars is God. I wanted to use the wire to represent the jar and to show that having God in my life is where my strength comes from. I then designed the top of the basket to resemble a crown of thorns." In the example stepped out here, Ruth added a button-stack charm that was made by Liz Smith.

Wire Basket

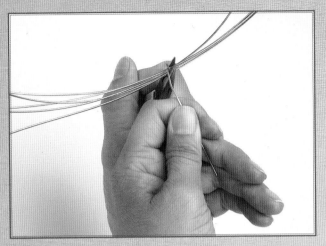

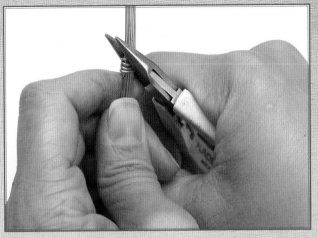

{1} BUNDLE WIRES TOGETHER

Twist enough 24-gauge wire to create 48" (122cm) of loosely twisted wire (see page 109 for instruction). Cut five pieces of 10½" (27cm) 18-gauge wire. Also cut a 3" (8cm) piece of 18-gauge wire. With the 10½" (27cm) pieces stacked, find the center and wrap the 3" (8cm) piece around them to secure. I start this wrap with a hook at one end of the wrapping wire.

{2} SECURE FIRMLY WITH WRAPPED WIRE

Wrap the wire about four times, and cut off the excess wrapping wire. Use the pliers to really smash the wrapping to hold it together tightly.

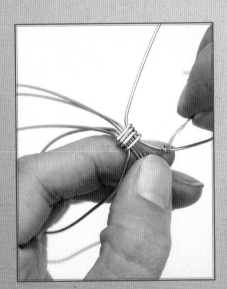

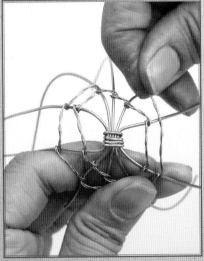

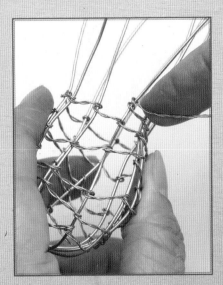

{3} SECURE WIRE TO BUNDLE

Begin curling the spokes up to form the general shape of the basket. Take the piece of twisted wire and wrap it around the base of one of the spokes.

{4} BEGIN WRAPPING WIRE

Start to make the basket by wrapping the twisted wire 360 degrees around each of the spokes, working in a spiral around the entire piece, from bottom to top.

{5} WORK BASKET EVENLY

As you continue working around and begin to shape the sides of the basket, keep the spokes evenly spaced and your tension consistent. When your basket is the desired height, finish by wrapping the wire one extra time around one of the spokes.

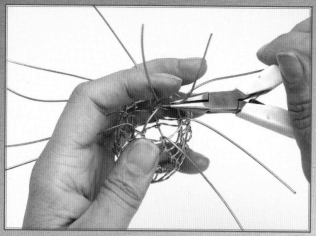

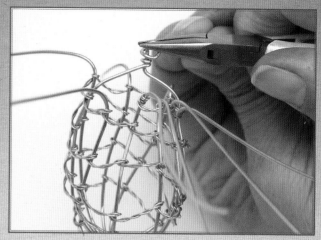

{6} SECURE TWO WIRES TOGETHER AT TOP

Trim the twisted wire with flush cutters. Choose two wires that are opposite one another. Bend one wire in toward the center, and then straight up. Bend the opposite wire toward the center and wrap it around the first wire.

{7} CREATE AN EYE AT CENTER

Trim the wrapping wire. Form the first wire into an eye and wrap the excess around the base of the loop over the first wrapping.

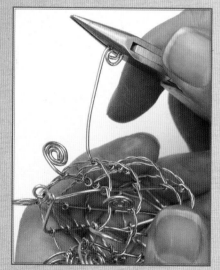

{8} COIL REMAINING WIRES

Trim the excess, if any. Trim the remaining spokes each to 2" (5cm). Starting with round-nose pliers, create a spiral on each piece. Switch to chain-nose pliers to coil each spiral down until it meets the basket.

{9} PREPARE DANGLING ELEMENT

Dip the basket and a 5" (13cm) piece of 20-gauge wire into liver of sulphur to blacken it. Rinse with vinegar and water and let dry. Use the piece of 5" (13cm) wire to create a rosary wrap (see page 110 for instruction) on the charm you wish to suspend from the basket.

{10} SECURE DANGLE TO BASKET

Wrap the end of the wire to the eye loop hanger at the top of the basket.

My talisman was created to bring safety to one's home and children. Nests are images representing family and love. A bird has created a safe home for her young. It brings strength and hope for the future. I have collected stones with holes in them throughout my life. They are traditionally thought of as lucky, and they bring me hope and comfort. May the strength of the stones and the love of the family always be with you.

—Martha

Home
{TALISMAN VII}
Martha Brown

This is a friendship talisman because most of the elements were made while experimenting with art with friends. My friend Melissa David taught several of us how to do the faux raku technique with polymer clay (the face). The etched copper wings were something I taught the group to do. And the patina/rusty pieces were done with bowls of solutions that we threw lots of metal pieces into. When I wear this necklace, I think of all the delightful times I have had playing with my art friends.

—Cece

Friendship
{TALISMAN VIII}
Cece Grimes

Found-object art involves the artistic use of something commonplace and ordinary that may be either manufactured or found in nature but is meant for another purpose. Marcel Duchamp originated this art movement in 1915 by calling a urinal an art piece and naming it Fountain. Our artists in this exchange were not nearly as shocking as Mr. Duchamp. But several unusal everyday items did find themselves surprisingly living the high life as lovely jewelry pieces. The players in this exchange were Jennifer Rowland, Cece Grimes, Ruth Rae, Lorraine George and me.

ONE WILD THOUGHT

KELLY SNELLING

MATERIALS

18-gauge brass wire

24-gauge wire

twisted-wire jump rings, 2
　(see page 112)

pre-made clasp

basic jewelry tools (see page 8)

assorted electrical items

hardware-store chain

paintbrush

gel medium

pearls and assorted beads

stone beads, 12

clipped book text

colored pencils (optional)

I have long been a collector of treasures (also known as trash by my husband). If I were to empty my pockets on any given day you would think I were a seven-year-old boy by the string, rocks, bottle caps and miscellanous debris I accumulate there. In addition to the brass chain I bought from a big spool at the hardware store, this piece has a metal switch and several metal bits that look like bubble blowers, originally intended for electrical use. These were all found in a salvage yard in Arizona, but you can find similar trinkets at your local hardware store. To balance out the shapes and metals, I added chunky faceted amethysts, tiny garnets, freshwater pearls and quartz.

Hardware Pendant

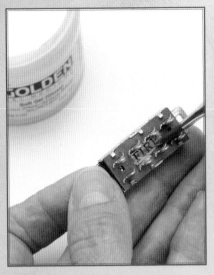

{1} LAY OUT ELEMENTS

Lay out your found objects to determine the general design, including a cut piece of text.

{2} ADHERE TEXT ELEMENT

Add a bit of color to your text if you like, using colored pencils. Then use a brush and some gel medium to adhere the text to the desired section of an electrical element.

{3} SECURE WIRE TO ELEMENT

Cut a length of 18-gauge brass wire to 6" (15cm) and thread it through the switch. Bend the wires up and toward the center and wrap one wire around the other.

{4} CREATE LOOP AND COMPLETE WRAP

Make a loop at the top of the wrap, using round-nose pliers, and then wrap again.

{5} CREATE AND ADD DANGLES

To create dangles, cut a 12" (30cm) length of 24-gauge wire. Thread on a bead and wrap the excess around the wire. Decide how long you want the dangle to be, and then make a loop. Thread the loop of the dangle onto the switch, and then wrap the tail up and down the length.

Connected Chains

{1} SECURE SEGMENTS WITH JUMP RINGS

Make eleven jump rings with 18-gauge wire. Rosary-wrap (see page 110 for instruction) eight stone beads and make two sections of four each, connecting them with jump rings on each side. Add a length of hardware-store chain to one end. Repeat for the other four stones, and add a clasp to one end of the chain.

Capacitator Charms

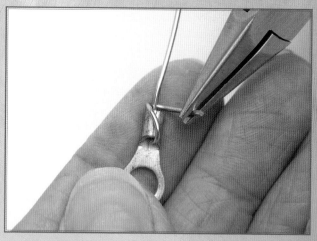

{1} SECURE WIRE TO ELECTRICAL ELEMENT

Create additional dangles using small electrical parts, such as capacitators, by wrapping brass wire through the channel.

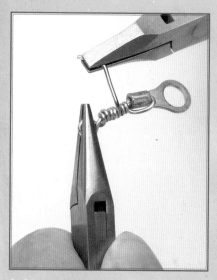

{2} CREATE EYE LOOP AND WRAP

Wrap the short end of the wire, and then create an eye loop and wrap the remaining wire.

{3} SECURE DANGLES TO ELEMENT

Create additional bead dangles to hang from a brass jump ring, and then attach the jump ring to the capacitor.

{4} ADD DANGLES TO JUMP RINGS

Repeat for five additional charms and attach one to each jump ring that is between two stones. Connect the two sides with one twisted jump ring. Then hang the switch pendant from a jump ring attached to the twisted jump ring.

I think this pendant is so fantastic. Cece Grimes flattened a silver spoon to turn it into an awesome charm with wings and watch parts. It inspired me to make this double-strand chain from galvanized aluminum and copper. I also added two sweet steel and mother-of-pearl charms made by Deryn Mentock. Then I gave it to Ruth, who darkened it with liver of sulphur to give it a more vintage, distressed look.

Time Flies II
{FOUND-OBJECT SWAP II}

**Cece Grimes, Deryn Mentock,
Ruth Rae** & **Kelly Snelling**

Animal Crackers

Jennifer Rowland

Found-Object Swap

MATERIALS

decorative tin

metal shears

disk cutter

hammer (optional)

two-hole punch or drill

$\frac{1}{16}$" (2mm) bit

rubber mallet

eyelet setter

file

$\frac{1}{16}$" (2mm) eyelets

The Animal Crackers necklace is made from a collectible Animal Crackers tin. Do you remember, as a kid, getting Animal Crackers in little red rectangular paper boxes with shoelace handles? They bring back fond memories for Jennifer Rowland, whose dad collected food and candy tins for many years. She recently purchased a metal disk cutter and had been searching for tin containers to use for jewelry making when he gave her

an Animal Crackers tin. She felt it would be perfect for creating numerous animal charms—each one different yet cohesive as a group. As she described it, "When I first saw the tin I had the *ah-ha!* moment—a necklace! The tin itself also had the animal names labeled, so I incorporated the name pieces to make even more whimsical charms." I think you'll agree that she made fine use of this nontraditional art supply.

Tin Charms

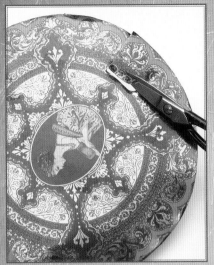

{1} CUT AWAY DESIRED SECTION
Remove a portion of a decorative tin (in this instance, it was the middle of the lid) and, using metal shears, cut out your desired shape.

{2} POSITION TIN IN CUTTER
To cut perfect circles, use a metal disk cutter. Use the cutter as a guide to decide from which section to cut your circle. (Note: Alternatively, you can cut out circles with metal shears and file the edges to soften them.)

{3} PUNCH TIN WITH HAMMER
Use a hammer and the punch to cut the circle from the tin.

{4} CREATE HOLES IN CIRCLES
For each charm, cut two sides. Holding the pieces together, punch three holes through both pieces.

{5} CUT OUT OTHER ELEMENTS
For the handcut pieces, don't worry too much about them being exactly the same size. Hammer both pieces with a rubber mallet.

{6} SECURE WITH EYELETS
Punch two holes in the piece, and then set an eyelet in each hole. Use metal shears to even up the two sides, and file the edges smooth.

High-Drama Vintage Lace

{FOUND-OBJECT SWAP IV}

Mija Marie & **Kelly Snelling**

Mija Marie takes collecting to a whole new level. On a regular basis, she will call to ask if I want to go in on a shipment of bug wings, mink bones or porcupine quills. We are kindred spirits. She also collects beautiful vintage lace, and she turned a piece of it into a necklace for me. I decided to add freshwater pearls and charms made of polymer clay, glass, collage images and silver leaf to give the necklace some additional high drama.

Ruth fell in love with Liz's happy button stack and added more buttons and the words *dream* and *free* before giving it a home on a strand of large bronze pearls and a leather cord. She also added two beaded sections of river rock that Liz had turned into beautiful organic elements. The result is one of subdued elegance.

Button Stack & Pearls
{Found-Object Swap v}
Ruth Rae & **Liz Smith**

Time Flies I

Cece Grimes, Jessica Moreau-Berry,
Kelly Snelling & Ruth Rae

Found-Object Swap

MATERIALS

18-gauge wire	paintbrush
jump rings, 3	copper bezel with
permanent marker	acrylic face
two-hole punch	epoxy
or drill	patina solution
1/16" (2mm) bit	large watch face
basic jewelry tools	safety pins
(see page 8)	brass wings charm
steel bench block	image for bezel
file	text tag
snips	metal

Cece Grimes sent us this awesome pendant with the framed flying baby-doll head. We immediately fell in love with it and wanted to feature it on a special piece. Ruth and I played with the design in Ruth's studio. We worked feverishly in a tag-team style, gathering freshwater pearls, long white vintage beads that I had found at my local antique flea market, a tender little charm from Jess and a mysterious little number 3 charm from Cece. Ruth worked her magic to cull all these elements into a striking necklace with a found-object point of view.

Watch-Face Pendant

{1} APPLY PATINA TO COPPER
Apply patina to the copper bezel, following manufacturer's instructions.

{2} MARK FOR HOLES
Use a permanent marker to mark where you want to make your holes for the dangles on the clock face.

{3} PUNCH HOLES AT MARKS
Drill or use a hole punch to make the holes.

{4} BEND IN PRONGS
Use pliers to bend the prongs of the clock face back.

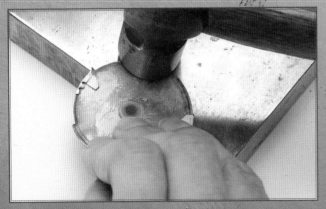

{5} HAMMER CLOCK FACE FLAT
Hammer the folded prongs nice and flat.

{6} FILE EDGES TO SMOOTH
If the edges are rough, file them a bit with a file.

{7} SECURE THREE SAFETY PINS

Hang three safety pins from three jump rings and attach them in the holes in the clock face.

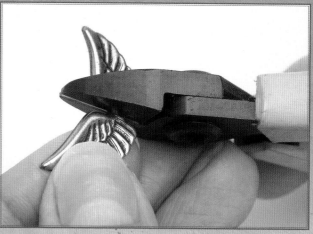

{8} DIVIDE WINGS INTO TWO

Cut a brass wing embellishment in half, using snips.

{9} SECURE IMAGE INTO BEZEL

Insert your acrylic piece and image into the copper bezel and fold in the prongs to hold everything in. (You may need to add a piece of cardstock to make the piece flush on the back and not rattle around.)

{10} ADHERE TEXT TAG

Glue a metal text tag to the watch face, using epoxy. Also adhere the bezel and the two wings to the piece.

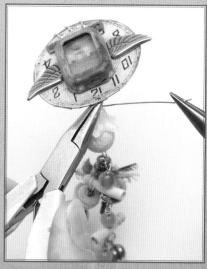

{11} ATTACH PENDANT

Attach the pendant to the necklace with a wire wrap, using 18-gauge wire.

Braided Bird

{FOUND-OBJECT SWAP VII}

Ruth Rae & **Mija Marie**

Mija cleverly used a vintage milk-bottle lid as the base for the pretty bird pendant. She painted it, stamped on a raven image and then used a silver paint pen to finish the embellishments. Ruth knotted seed beads onto silk cord, braided them with ribbon and finished it all off with a silver clasp.

Tire-Swing Babies

Lou McCulloch, Ruth Rae & Kelly Snelling

MATERIALS

16-gauge wire

20-gauge copper wire

24-gauge wire

.062 piano wire or 1/16" (2mm)
    mandrel

1/4" (6mm) dowel or mandrel

basic jewelry tools (see page 8)

drill and 1/16" (2mm) bit

jeweler's saw

steel bench block

rusting solution

paintbrush

tiny plastic babies

iron paint

By the time we got to the making of this necklace, Ruth and I were in the middle of a blazing California summer working in an un-air-conditioned garage. Ah, yes, art is so glamorous. Perhaps that explains the wild (aka delirious) inspiration that led to the Tire-Swing Babies necklace. Ruth, like most mixed-media artists, enjoys scouring her local thrift stores in search of trinkets and baubles to use in her work. She happened upon a slew of tiny plastic babies and knew they would come into play one way or another. I walked in, saw the babies and decided we should rust them. Next, we added Lou McCulloch's cool pendant made from an old key, and the rest came from the mind of Ruth, who put them all together with a swinging, found-object twist.

Coiled Jump Rings

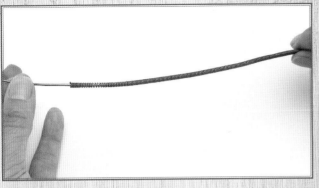

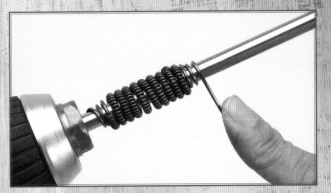

{1} THREAD A LONG COIL
Create a long coil of 20-gauge copper wire using a ¹⁄₁₆" (2mm) mandrel and a drill. Thread a length of 16-gauge wire through the coil.

{2} WRAP COIL AROUND MANDREL
Secure the two together into a drill and coil them around a ¼" (6mm) mandrel. Saw the coil apart into individual rings and set them aside.

Double-Loop Link

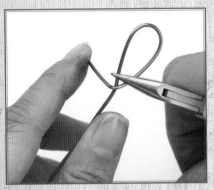

{1} CREATE FIRST LOOP
Cut a 6½" (17cm) length of 16-gauge wire. Create a loop at one end, and wrap the excess around the base.

{2} CREATE SECOND LOOP
Wrap the remaining wire in the opposite direction for a second loop, and wrap the end around the base again. Trim any excess.

{3} HAMMER LOOPS FLAT
Hammer the entire link flat, and then add some texture with the ball side of the hammer.

{4} LINK TOGETHER WITH COILED JUMP RINGS
Repeat steps 1–3 to create twelve more links. Assemble the chain by alternating coiled jump rings and double-loop links.

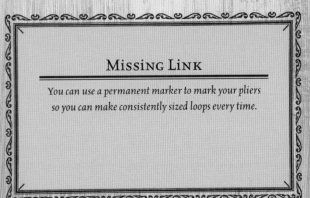

MISSING LINK
You can use a permanent marker to mark your pliers so you can make consistently sized loops every time.

Baby-Swing Links

{1} PREPARE BABIES WITH PAINT

To create the baby-swing elements, start by drilling a hole through the seat of the baby from one side to the other, using a $\frac{1}{16}$" (2mm) drill bit. Lightly sand and then paint the plastic babies with iron paint.

{2} ADD RUSTING SOLUTION

When the paint is dry, brush on the rusting solution liberally.

{3} CREATE LOOP AT SEAT

To make a "swing" for the baby, begin with a 4" (10cm) length of 24-gauge wire. Thread the length of wire through the hole in the baby, and create a wire-wrapped loop at the center of the baby seat.

{4} CREATE SWING SEAT AND SIDES

Create about a 2" (5cm) coil from 24-gauge wire, using a piano-wire mandrel. Cut the coil into four $\frac{1}{2}$" (13mm) sections. Cut a 9" (23cm) length of 24-gauge wire and thread it through the seat of the baby, centering it. Thread a coil piece onto each half of the wire. Twist the wire around each hand of the baby.

{5} SECURE SWING AT TOP

Bring the wire ends together at the top and twist together. Create an eye loop on one wire, and wrap the ends to complete.

Lorraine started her found-object necklace with an oxidized commercial chain. To this she added several dangly seed bead and crystal segments along with tiny bells and more chain. But the amazing feature of this necklace is that Lorraine created a gorgeous focal bead and smaller elements from bullet casings. You would never know that's what they are made from.

Another word for *creativity* **is courage.**

—George Prince

CREATE & COLLABORATE

To enjoy a successful, artistic collaboration, artists should be unafraid of failure, open to the ideas of others and willing to persistently take risks. That sounds sort of starchy and formal, so let me break it down,

Fear will stop you in your tracks and kill your creative impulses. Art is supposed to be whatever you want it to be—you cannot fail and you get to dictate your own rules. I often remind myself to get out of my own way. I suggest you do the same; let go of all inhibitions and create with ridiculous amounts of glee.

With jewelry, I find it helpful to see it worn. I've had my kids wearing my jewelry many more times than they would have liked (I have two sons). But if they aren't willing to help, I will put the piece on and stand in front of the mirror. It gives a different perspective and allows me to look at the piece with new eyes.

When you decide to create collaboratively, looking at something anew becomes even more important because you are working with others who may have a completely different set of ideas about how a piece of jewelry works. Much of these processes go unnoticed when one is working alone. So it is a good idea to think about and communicate your expectations for the project with one another up front. It is much easier to have a successful endeavor if all the players share common intentions from the get-go. This can be as loose of a matter as determining that you all want to grow, learn new techniques and have fun. Or you may decide to be more specific and dictate exactly how long each person has to work on a piece, if the theme is open to interpretation or should be strictly adhered to, how much everyone should spend on materials and how many elements each artist should create. As long as everyone is on the same page, you are more likely to be free to create with abandon and to be satisfied with the results.

After all, one of the motivating factors in collaboration is the longing to create something new and to share this with others. The new creation may be the piece of art, or it may be the process and techniques used to arrive at the finished product.

When you open yourself up to the aspect of creating fearlessly, you will discover powerful possibilities of expression. And if you can do this while working with others who share your daring, the opportunities for shifting ideas, gaining riveting experiences and taking giant artistic leaps are boundless.

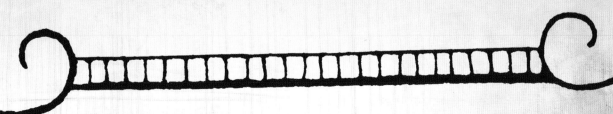

Bright Idea

Lorraine George, Crystal Neubauer & Ruth Rae

The collaborative earrings you'll find on this and the following pages were some of the most fun projects we created for this book. Each pair was a collaboration between three artists.

Three girls each started one pair of earrings that would then be mailed, in turn, to the other two artists within the group until everyone had worked on all three pairs. We had new techniques appear in this project as well as a swarm of renegade materials, which we had grown to expect with our no-holds-barred group of artists. In addition to beautiful beads and sterling chain, these pairs of earrings included such unusual elements as rivets dug from the desert, old resin-coated Bible pages and toy jacks.

In this first pair, Crystal Neubauer (a found-object super-star) started her earrings by skillfully caging a miniature light bulb with wire. Then, they traveled on to Lorraine George. Lorraine said she wasn't sure what to do with them until she saw the blue filament in one and a bluish tint to part of the brass on another. She added a beautiful peacock-blue pearl and brass accents to tone down the softness of the pearl and complement the industrious light bulb.

Lastly, Ruth got a turn with these. She cut out brass circles and then dapped them to form bowls. She drilled small holes into the bowls, and for a final decorative finish, she hung a little pearl in each one.

Three-Tier Earrings

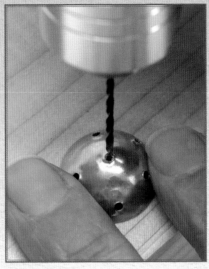

{1} DAP BRASS INTO BOWLS
Cut a circle from a piece of 24-gauge brass sheet, using shears or a disk cutter. Use a dapping block to create a bowl shape from the disk. Create two bowls.

{2} DRILL HOLES IN BOWLS
Drill six holes in each bowl. Set the bowls aside. Lightly sand holes on both sides.

{3} CREATE SPIRAL
For the tiny light bulbs, cut a length of 20-gauge wire to 9" (23cm). Leave a 1" (3cm) tail, and bend the wire at 90 degrees. Spiral the wire from the bend out until you have about five rotations.

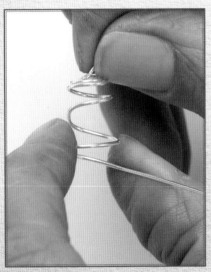

{4} SPREAD SPIRAL OUT
With the tail, create a small eye. Expand the spiral into a coil.

{5} WRAP WIRE AROUND BULB
Push the bulb into the coil and work the wire to the shape of the bulb. Wrap the wire around the threaded part of the bulb.

{6} ASSEMBLE EARRINGS
Cut a 3" (8cm) piece of 24-gauge wire. Thread a 3mm bead onto the wire and bring the wire around it in a U shape. Wrap the wire where the sections of it come together, and then insert the end of the wire through one of the holes in the bowl. Create a second eye outside the bowl with the remaining wire. Create a rosary-wrapped section of beads and attach it to the bottom of the bulb and to the eye on the bowl. Attach an ear wire to the top of the bulb.

Collaborative Earrings

Each of the pairs of earrings on these two pages was worked on by three separate artists.

We have an amazing monthly antiques flea market in my town. There's a fellow there who sells fascinating treasures that he digs up in the desert. That's where I got the elements that I used to begin my earrings. They are rusty rivets that once graced a pair of miner's blue jeans. I used a metal punch to put holes in them and then sent them off to Deryn. Clever girl that she is, Deryn used turquoise stones to book-end little bundles of transparent Bible pages that she had created by coating them with resin. And Maija created her finishing touch by using copper mesh and eyelets to make a tiny, dangling charm.

Kelly Snelling, Deryn Mentock & Maija Lepore
{Group I}

Deryn wanted her collaborative pair of earrings to be asymmetrical. So, after fashioning some pretty ear wires she added a dental crown to one and an old watch face to the other. Maija got these next and wasted no time creating sweet little additions by using parts of an old sewing bobbin backed with text and crystals. By the time I got them I didn't want to do anything that would take way from what was already there. The other elements made strong statements already. I must have bought seventeen different things for these. In the end I used tiny faceted labradorite gems to embellish the beautiful earrings.

Maija started her earrings with a pair of playground jacks. When she sent them to me I decided to wire wrap two of each jack's arms and add small, faceted, smoky quartz briolettes and tiny pearls. Next, the earrings went to Deryn, who added some excellent little skull beads carved from bone.

Jennifer started this collaborative pair of earrings with hammered metal disks topped with a faceted crystal and a piece of cloth measuring tape. Liz then decided to dangle from these even smaller metal disks, a bead and a bell-shaped charm. Dawn completed the trio of artists, and the earrings, with a creative wire wrap and small green bead.

Jennifer Rowland, Liz Smith & Dawn Supina
{Group II}

Cece Grimes, Debra Cooper & Sally Turlington
{Group III}

Cece introduced her earrings with a red metal rectangle to which she added eyelets and circle links. Debra came in and added pretty clusters of red beads and a small heart charm to each earring. Sally was the last to work on this pair. She cleverly added Cece's initials with typewriter keys and little silver hand charms.

Sally started off her earrings with a roar. She added a large snap to one earring and a black zipper pull to the other before sending them off to Cece. They were met with squeals of approval. Cece even considered keeping them because "they totally rock in a biker-chick kind of way!" she said. She added three small black snaps in descending sizes, along with some little safety pins. By the time Debra got to add her additions, she knew just what to do. She added some extra zip by embellishing the safety pins with silver beads and a little spring.

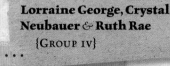

Debra began her earrings by attaching a brass floral charm to her ear wires. When Sally got them, she added a painted metal disc and created an angel in acrylics. A cross dangle completed the middle section of these. Cece spiced them up further by adding a red glass heart bead to Debra's original charm. She then finished them off with a freshwater pearl and spiral dangle.

Lorraine George, Crystal Neubauer & Ruth Rae
{Group IV}

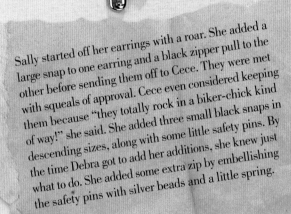

Lorraine started her earrings with a simple precious metal clay disk with long, silver chain attached. Ruth added pearls along with sea-colored stones that she tied onto the chain with silk beading thread. Then Crystal finished up the pair with lovely red wire-wrapped coral.

Ruth began this glamorous set of earrings with a faceted amethyst surrounded by a lavender stream of tiny freshwater pearls. Crystal took these and added an amber-colored bead segment. Then Lorraine came in to tie it all together with some pretty dangling chain finished with glittering beads.

Asymmetrical Earrings

Kelly Snelling

MATERIALS

24-gauge half-hard wire

⅝" (16mm) dowel

jump ring

basic jewelry tools

file

2" (5cm) eye pin

vintage jewelry parts

large pearl and large bead

The idea for this project is to have several artists team up to create pairs of earrings that are asymmetrical. There should be something about the two earrings that are similar, such as the color, theme or type of stones, but they should not be exactly the same. As a collaborative swap, everyone walks away with a set of whimsical earrings to keep for herself.

When we tried this, we worked in pairs. Each artist chose a theme or color palette for her earrings. Each then made one earring and sent it to her partner. She could also send along some elements for her partner to use in the other earring or leave it up to her to find complementary items to go with the original. This was a great opportunity for the artists to raid their vintage and costume jewelry stashes. If you had an extraordinary set of earrings that your grandma gave you, but you lost one, this was your chance to work it into a new piece.

I like things a little more outlandish and funky than Ruth does. I think it is fine if one of the earrings is longer than the other. Ruth prefers things to match a little more, but I think this entire project loosened her up a bit. What you create is up to you and your partner. Let this project be about the process, and have a ball!

Single Earring

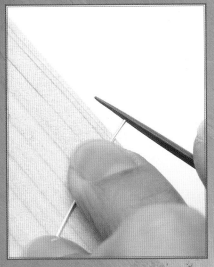

{1} TRIM AND FILE WIRE
Cut a 3" (8cm) piece of 24-gauge wire. Using round-nose pliers, create a small eye loop at one end, and file the other end with a file so that it's no longer sharp.

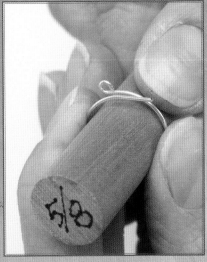

{2} CURVE WIRE INTO SHAPE
Starting at the eye end, bend the wire around a 5/8" (16mm) dowel.

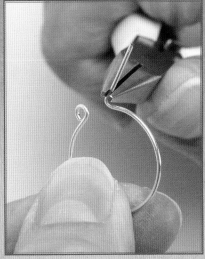

{3} BEND END BACK
Bend the wire outward just past where it would overlap.

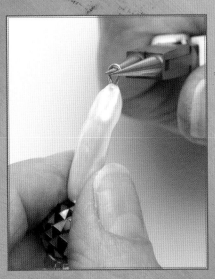

{4} THREAD BEADS ONTO PIN
Thread a 2" (5cm) eye pin with a large bead and a pearl. Make a second eye on the other end of the pin.

{5} ADD VINTAGE ELEMENT
Use a jump ring to connect a vintage jewelry piece to one end of the eye pin.

{6} ADD BEADS TO EAR WIRE
Attach the entire piece to the ear wire. Then repeat the process for the other earring, but substitute slightly different beads.

Asymmetrical Earring Swap

There were a lot of people who participated in this swap! As you can see, the sky's the limit when it comes to creative ideas for earrings.

Fiona Mortimore & **Cece Grimes**

Ruth Rae & **Marci Glenn**

Edina Tien & **Liz Smith**

A friend and I got together last night to make earrings. I ended up making four pairs of asymmetrical earrings! At first it was difficult to get my brain in the mode, but I gradually worked through it. One pair in particular was especially funky. Even my friend, who must have everything match, loved them. I am looking forward to working on a pair with a partner from our art group!

—*Dawn Supina*

Deryn Mentock & **Dot Christian**

I have always wanted to make earrings like these. I have been saving some jewelry parts, so I do want to join in the fun. I think I am going to be so into earrings now that I'll be bald soon. This is too perfect!

—*Joanna Pierotti*, preparing to start chemotherapy

Mija Marie & **Debra Cooper**

Jennifer Rowland & **Dawn Supina**

Joanna Pierotti & **Kelly Snelling**

Sally Turlington & **Marci Glenn**

Ruth Rae

Mija Marie & Debra Cooper

Ruth Rae

Ruth Rae & Marci Glenn

Crystal Neubauer & Maija Lepore

Ruth Rae

Sally Turlington & **Ruth Rae**

Ruth Rae & **Maija Lepore**

Jennifer Rowland & **Ruth Rae**

Ruth Rae & **Liz Smith**

Sugar 'n Spice Bracelet

Holly Stinnett, Michael Johansson & Ruth Rae

MATERIALS

detail scissors

1/8" (3mm) hole punch

eyelet setter

hammer

steel bench block

dimensional adhesive

doll-head images

black cardstock

1/8" (3mm) eyelets

When Holly Stinnett was a little girl she had some great paper dolls. She even had some much coveted vintage Barbie ones that had belonged to her mother. Now Holly's a grown-up girl, and she very cleverly used her old paper dolls to make the cutest charms for a bracelet. We think they are incredible. They completely remind me of the 1970s. Ruth contacted Michael Johansson, a polymer clay artist whose work she had admired online, and she delivered a tiny treasure trove of freshly-baked charms to sweeten up the whole deal. Michael makes miniature clay versions of food that you will swear are good enough to eat. I don't know how she does it, but they are amazing. Ruth added Holly's and Michael's charms to a store-bought chain with some darling dotted glass beads that look like little lanterns. I think this bracelet is beyond adorable! You could even make a version of these charms with pictures of your family members, your pets or your child and his classmates for a special teacher gift.

Doll-Head Charm

{1} ADHERE IMAGE TO CARDSTOCK
Glue an image of a doll head to a piece of black cardstock, using some dimensional adhesive such as Diamond Glaze.

{2} CUT OUT SHAPE
Precisely cut out the shape with detail scissors.

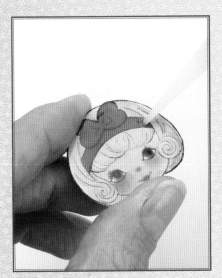

{3} SEAL BOTH SIDES
Squeeze a generous amount of Diamond Glaze over both sides.

{4} PUNCH HOLE
When the piece is dry, punch a hole through the top with a ⅛" (3mm) punch.

{5} SET EYELET IN HOLE
Set a ⅛" (3mm) eyelet in the hole, using an eyelet setter and hammer.

Seashore Bracelet

Ruth Rae, Kelly Snelling, Fiona Mortimore, Cece Grimes & Lelainia Lloyd

MATERIALS

18-gauge wire

³⁄₈" (10mm) dowels, 2

basic jewelry tools (see page 8)

steel bench block

vise

drill and ¹⁄₁₆" (2mm) bit

shell (such as clam)

6mm beads, 8

If you hold this bracelet to your ear, not only will you hear the ocean, but you will look devastatingly chic while doing it. Ruth made this feminine, sea-themed gem with charms created by Fiona Mortimore, Cece Grimes, Lelainia Lloyd and me. That brought together the seas of Australia, Canada and the United States, which is like a grand holiday in and of itself. The girls used shells, pearls, a tiny sea star, glass glitter and a metal token that must be good for a fantasy ride across the seven seas. Ruth also created some fabulous links. I don't know how she comes up with so many wonderful design ideas, but she never fails to surprise me and take my breath away. I can't wait to make these links myself!

Decorative-Swirl Links

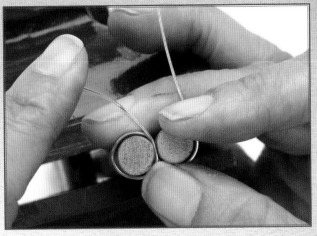

{1} WRAP WIRES IN OPPOSITE DIRECTIONS

Cut a length of 18-gauge wire to 5" (13cm). Secure two ⅜" (10mm) dowels in a vise and center the wire between them. Bring the two ends of the wire around in opposite directions.

{2} BRING WIRE TO CENTER

Take one wire around all the way to the center.

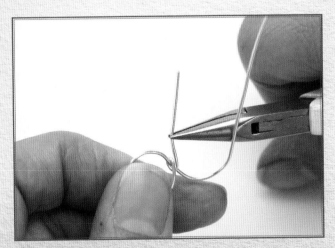

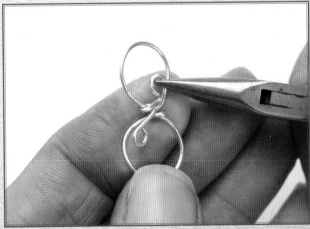

{3} WRAP WIRE IN CENTER

Remove the wire from the dowels and wrap the wire around the center.

{4} CURL IN WIRE ENDS

Flip the piece over and repeat for the other wire, wrapping it in the opposite direction. Then wrap that wire around the center as well. Trim the tails to ½" (13mm) from the outside of the circles. Create a loop on the end of each tail (make each in an opposite direction) and then bend each up into the two circles. Hammer the loops and then repeat to make a total of nine links. (Note: Hammering the wires where they cross can weaken a piece, so try to avoid those areas and hammer only the loops.).

Swirl Clasp

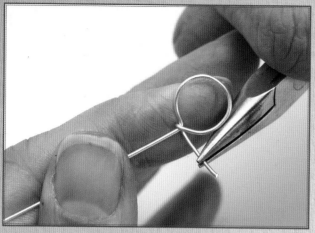

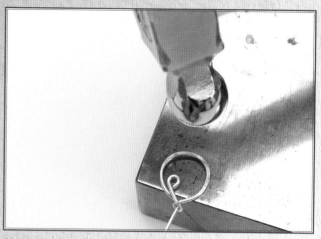

{1} CREATE LARGE LOOP

To create a hook, cut 6" (15cm) of 18-gauge wire and wrap it around the ⅜" (10mm) dowel about 1½" (4cm) from the end. Wrap the tail around the base of the large loop.

{2} HAMMER LOOP

After wrapping it one and a half times, create a tiny loop on the end of the wire and bend it up into the circle. Hammer the loop.

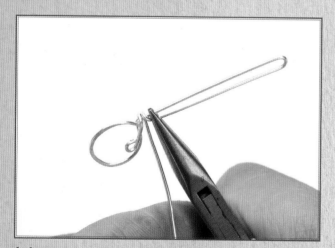

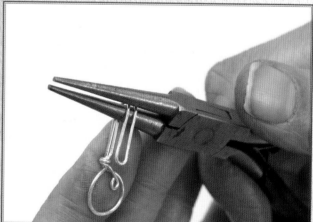

{3} BEND WIRE AND WRAP AT BASE

At 2" (5mm) from the circle, bend the wire, and wrap the wire at the base of the circle.

{4} BEND WIRE TO FORM HOOK

Trim the excess from the tail if needed. Then create a hook from the folded piece, using the round-nose pliers. (Bend the tip of the hook back a bit to complete it.)

Shell Charm

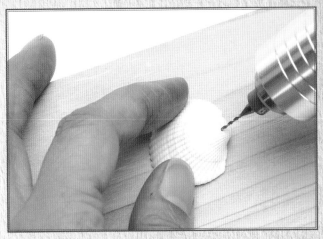

{1} DRILL HOLE IN SHELL
To create a shell charm, begin by drilling a hole at the base of it.

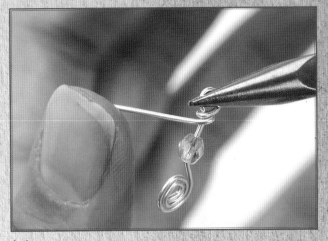

{2} CREATE BEAD-AND-SWIRL DANGLE
Cut five to seven pieces of 18-gauge wire that are about 3" (8cm) in length. Spiral the end of one piece for about four turns and then bend the wire up a bit and thread on a 6mm bead. On the other side of the bead, create an eye and wire wrap.

{3} THREAD DANGLES ON WIRE LOOP
Repeat step 2 to create four additional dangles. Cut 3" (8cm) of 18-gauge wire, and make a loop on one end. Thread on the swirl dangles, and then wrap the wire to close it.

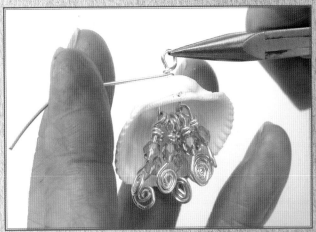

{4} CREATE EYE LOOP AT TOP OF SHELL
Thread the wire through the shell from the inside to the outside. Create another loop at the top of the shell and wrap the tail around that as well.

CREATE ART BRACELET

RUTH RAE, KELLY SNELLING, CATHERINE WITHERELL, JESSICA MOREAU-BERRY, DERYN MENTOCK & CRYSTAL NEUBAUER

MATERIALS

coated beading wire and corresponding crimp beads	bench pin
	drill
	1/16" (2mm) bit
24-gauge silver sheet	text rubber stamp
2-13mm jump rings	fast-acting
basic jewelry tools (see page 8)	bonding glue
	clear nail polish
crimping pliers	or epoxy
scissors	leather
1/8" (3mm) hole punch	organza ribbon
	assorted beads
eyelet setter	1/8" (3mm) eyelets, 3
sewing needle	premade toggle clasp
thread	permanent marker
jeweler's saw	black ink (StazOn)
metal alphabet stamp set	

Not long after we started working on this book, I discovered I had breast cancer. Ruth pulled together the girls from the round-robin group to make a special keepsake bracelet to lift my spirits, to encourage me and to remind me that I am loved.

When a piece was chosen for the cover of this book, my beautiful bracelet was brought out once again. But rather than make me part with my special gift for many months, we made a similar version and I contributed a charm to go along with this one.

Our friend Joanna Pierotti was also fighting breast cancer during the making of this book. With so many pieces in the book being collaborative, and knowing that deciding who would get what when the book was complete would be difficult, we all agreed that the collaborative pieces would be auctioned to raise money for breast-cancer research. If you are interested in buying this spectacular bracelet or some of the other gorgeous pieces in this book, stay tuned to our book blog (www.acharmingexchange.blogspot.com) and personal websites listed on page 125 for more information.

Beads & Ribbon Bracelet

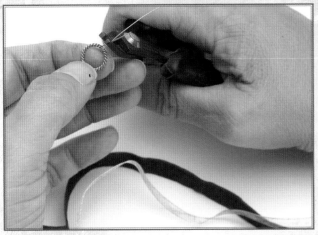

{1} SECURE WIRE TO JUMP RING

Cut a strip of leather and a piece of organza ribbon to 8" (20cm). Cut two pieces of coated wire to 8½" (22cm). Attach one piece of coated wire to a 13mm jump ring, using a crimp bead.

{2} SECURE RIBBON AND LEATHER TOGETHER

String a length of assorted beads/pearls onto the wire until it is the desired length for your bracelet. Then attach the other end to the other jump ring, using another crimp bead. Stamp the length of organza ribbon with a text stamp, using black StazOn ink. Secure the ribbon and the leather together by setting an eyelet through both layers in the center and at 1" (3cm) from each end.

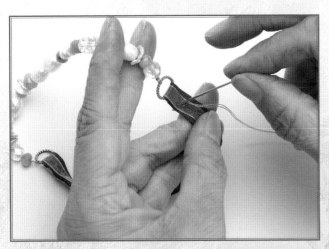

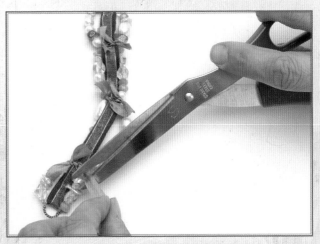

{3} SEW LEATHER THROUGH JUMP RING

Secure the leather piece to the jump ring by threading it through about ½" (13mm) and using fast-acting bonding glue to secure it to the back of itself. Then handsew it to further secure it. Attach the piece to the jump ring at the other end the same way.

{4} TIE BRACELET WITH RIBBON PIECES

Cut six 4" (10cm) lengths of organza ribbon. Thread two pieces through the first hole, and tie one piece to a beaded strand on each side of the leather strip. Apply a dab of clear nail polish or epoxy to each knot for added security, and trim the ribbon ends. Add a commercial toggle clasp to the jump rings.

Tree Charm

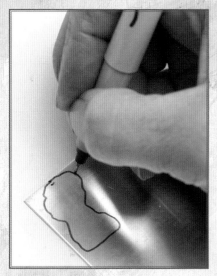

{1} SKETCH TREE SHAPE
To create a tree charm, start with a 24-gauge piece of silver sheet. Sketch out your desired shape, using a permanent marker.

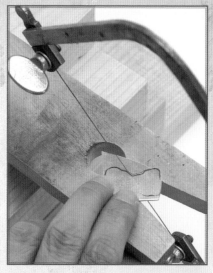

{2} CUT OUT SHAPE WITH SAW
Working on a bench pin and using a jeweler's saw, saw out the shape.

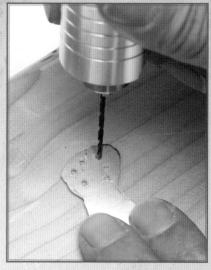

{3} DRILL HOLES AT TREE TOP
Drill five to seven holes into the foliage portion of the tree, using a $\frac{1}{16}$" (2mm) bit.

{4} CUT BRANCH LINES
To create the branches of the tree, first unlatch the saw blade and insert it through one of the holes, and then reattach. Cut a free-form series of lines for the trunk portion, and then remove the blade and repeat in each of the remaining holes to cut branches.

{5} ADD TEXTURE WITH HAMMER
Add texture to the charm by hammering it with a ball-peen and a cross-peen hammer. The ball peen will give the piece round indentations for leaves, while the cross peen will create lines for the bark. Use letter stamps and a hammer to spell out *art*.

{6} ATTACH CHARMS TO BRACELET
Create a wire wrap for the charm, and attach it to the bracelet. (Note: Other charms can be attached with jump rings or wire wraps.)

Ruth took lovely faceted ovals of smokey quartz and copper to create a bracelet for delightful charms from Deborah Edwards, Judith Thibaut and myself. Deborah hammered a copper oval with a ball-peen hammer before pounding in the word *divine*. I adhered a transparency image onto a copper disk and used a gold paint pen to highlight it. Lastly, Judith stitched a vintage German postage stamp onto muslin for a little pillow charm and used a vintage brass heart for her second.

Divine

Ruth Rae, Deborah Edwards, Kelly Snelling & **Judith Thibaut**

Button Bracelet

Ruth Rae, Lelainia Lloyd, Jessica Moreau-Berry, Lou McCulloch,
Cece Grimes, Jennifer Rowland, Martha Brown & Maija Lepore

MATERIALS

24-gauge wire

precut jump rings

basic jewelry tools

drill and ¹⁄₁₆" (2mm) bit

paintbrush

gel medium

assorted buttons

thimble

assorted fibers

clipped piece of text

Ruth has cases and cases of the most amazingly gorgeous gemstones that she has collected over her many years of jewelry making. And she generously shared them for all these projects the entire summer. Take this piece, for instance. Lelainia sent us this gorgeous button strand from her collection, which inspired Ruth to make this pretty bracelet. But let me tell you, take one look at her mason jars brimming over with tiny vintage buttons, and she breaks out in a sweat. Her heart rate visibly increases. Little buttons, especially old mother-of-pearl

buttons, are better than diamonds to Ruth. And it would seem she is not alone. We had quite a few fabric artists in our merry band who made sewing-inspired charms. So if you have collected buttons from your grandmother, or saved little thimbles from your great aunt Ethel, here is a special bracelet for you to create to show them off in a manner befitting the riches they truly are.

Strand of Buttons   Thimble Charm

  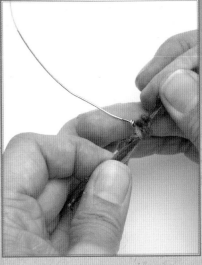

{1} CONNECT BUTTONS
It's easy to create a bracelet with buttons: Simply connect them with precut jump rings through their holes.

{1} DRILL HOLE IN THIMBLE
To create a tasseled-thimble charm, start by drilling a ¹⁄₁₆" (2mm) hole into the top of a thimble.

{2} CREATE LOOP OF FIBERS
Cut a 3" (8cm) piece of 24-gauge wire and about five assorted fiber pieces to 2" (5cm). Make an eye loop at one end of the wire, and tie the fibers onto the loop.

{3} TRIM EXCESS FIBERS
Thread the wire through the hole in the thimble and make a wire-wrapped eye at the top. Trim the fibers to just slightly longer than the length of the thimble.

{4} ADHERE TEXT ELEMENT
Adhere a word onto the thimble, using a brush and gel medium. Apply additional medium over the top to seal the paper.

{5} ATTACH CHARM
Attach the thimble charm to the bracelet, using a jump ring.

Fiona Mortimore, Maija Lepore, Ruth Rae, Kelly Snelling, Kathy Wasilewski & Debra Cooper

This bracelet is perfect for a little princess or a grown-up one. Ruth used pink felt and pom-poms to create the base. Then she added a decorative clasp, and I stitched on several charms from Fiona Mortimore, Maija Lepore, Kathy Wasilewski, Debra Cooper and myself. This would even be a relatively easy first project for a young jeweler-in-training.

Jeweled Autumn

Mija Marie & Kelly Snelling

Mija Marie makes beautiful creations in a plethora of mediums, but her felted pieces are especially amazing. She sent in some awesome felted and beaded leaf charms that inspired me to make this chunky hammered cuff, which is wired with jewel-toned gemstones.

'50s Delight

Holly Stinnett, Michael Johansson & Ruth Rae

This bracelet is another take on Holly's, Michael's and Ruth's magic. Holly used copies of her mom's old paper dolls to create these sophisticated lady charms. Michael made Pop-Tarts and chocolate-chip cookies, complete with little bites taken out of them. Ruth put them all together with a store-bought chain, rhinestones and sparkling girly beads for this hit from the 1950s.

Secret Sky
Ruth Rae, Lou McCulloch & Catherine Witherell

Ruth strung a lovely mix of blue beads to remind her of the sky- and cloud-colored pearls to form this bracelet. While you can't see it in this photo, she used metal stamps to hammer the words *Secret Sky* into a silver bar. Then, she added some gorgeous charms from Catherine and Lou to complete this breezy bracelet.

This bracelet is a party for your wrist! The bright red beads are so happy that they will cheer up even the gloomiest of days. And, with the double strand of heart links and a constant reminder to PLAY, you will be sure to have a fantastic time whenever you put this one on.

The Game of Love
Ruth Rae, Maija Lepore, Jennifer Rowland, Cece Grimes & Judy Scott

Leather & Lace
Ruth Rae, Jennifer Rowland, Judy Scott, Joanna Pierotti & Liz Smith

Ruth fashioned this delicate bracelet from cheery vintage lace. She used a favorite antique mother-of-pearl buckle for the closure. Then she stitched on a special selection of charms that worked perfectly to create just the right balance for this pretty, vintage-inspired piece.

THE FABRIC ORBS

Jade Pegler & Ruth Rae

MATERIALS

18-gauge copper wire

24-gauge copper wire

⅝" (16mm) dowel

¼" (6mm) dowel

basic jewelry tools (see page 8)

awl

sewing machine (or needle
    and thread to handsew)

clear spray sealer

liver of sulphur

muslin

batting

assorted pearls and beads

permanent marker

colored pencil

Jade Pegler is a unique Australian artist. Her work is extremely evocative and original. In her series titled *Proscenium Machinium*, of which I am fond, she combines quilting, bookbinding, collage and papier mâché to create sculptures that, to me, resemble iconic beings from another world. They resonate with me. The works are monochromatic, surprising and unexpectedly tender.

Ruth met Jade online after long admiring her work. She approached her to make some fabric pieces for our book, and, to our good fortune, Jade agreed.

For this particular piece, she sent us four roughly cut muslin charms with a marvelous abstract drawing on each. We took to calling them orbs, although only one is round. The word just seemed to fit, so they became part of this beautiful necklace known as The Fabric Orbs.

Ruth wanted to create some very special links to reflect and enhance the unconventional aspect of the orbs. I think her copper-wire spheres are the perfect complement. The freshwater pearls resemble orbiting planets pulled in by a powerful attraction to Jade's amazing orbs.

Stuffed & Colored Links

{1} CREATE IMAGE ON MUSLIN
With a permanent marker, make a drawing on a piece of muslin.

{2} COLOR IN IMAGE
Color it lightly with colored pencil.

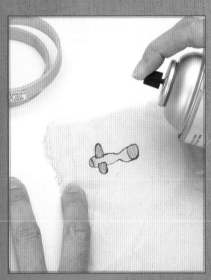

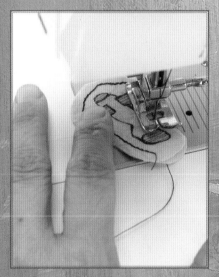

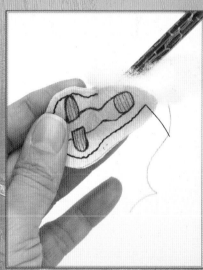

{3} SEAL IMAGE
Seal the piece with a light coat of spray sealer.

{4} SEW SIDES TOGETHER
Fold the fabric to create another layer under the image, and cut a loose, general shape around the drawing. Sew around the perimeter of the shape, leaving a small opening.

{5} STUFF WITH BATTING
Add a small amount of batting. A pencil eraser or chopstick works well to push the batting into hard-to-reach areas.

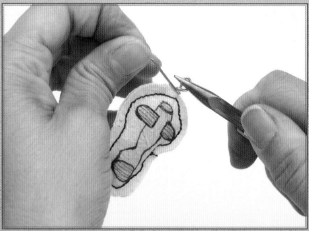

{6} MAKE PILOT HOLE

Sew the shape closed on the sewing machine. Use an awl to make a pilot hole through the stuffed shape.

{7} ADD WIRE TO STUFFED PIECE

Cut a 3½" (9cm) piece of 18-gauge wire, and make a rosary wrap on one end. Thread the wire through the stuffed piece, and then make a wrap on the other end.

Jump-Rings Connection

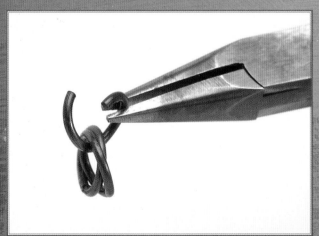

{1} LINK THREE JUMP RINGS

Create forty-four jump rings from 18-gauge wire by coiling it around a ¼" (6mm) dowel and cutting them apart with a jeweler's saw. Begin by interlocking two jump rings. Then add a third jump ring through the middle of those two.

{2} CONNECT ORBS WITH JUMP RINGS

Onto the same jump ring, thread one orb. Thread another jump ring through the first two jump rings and attach it to a second orb on the opposite side. Continue connecting the orbs with jump rings. Add a pendant of your choice.

Wire-Orb Links

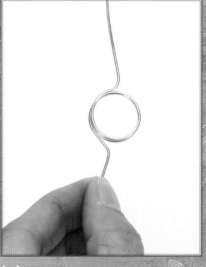

{1} WRAP WIRE AROUND DOWEL
Cut an 8" (20cm) length of 18-gauge wire and wrap it around a ⅝" (16mm) dowel three times.

{2} BEND OUT BOTH ENDS
Bend each end out at noon and six o'clock.

{3} SECURE COIL
Trim the wire ends to about 1" (3cm) each. Use chain-nose pliers to hold the coil at one bend, and wrap the wire around the coil. Repeat for the second end.

{4} SECURE COILING WIRE
Separate the coils slightly and, with a length of 24-gauge wire (about 12" [30cm]), coil it around one wire of the coil.

{5} ADD A BEAD
Wrap the wire around the entire circle a couple of times, and thread on a bead.

{6} FINISH WRAPPING
Continue wrapping the wire around the circle to secure it around the bundle of wires a couple of times, adding a second, smaller bead. Trim the excess. Repeat steps 1–6 to create seven more orbs.

Wire-Orb Clasp

{1} BEND WIRE FOR HOOK

To create a clasp, follow the directions for a wire orb. At step 3, trim the six o'clock tail and wrap as before, but leave the noon tail about 4" (10cm). Wrap the 24-gauge wire around the orb in the same fashion as before, including the addition of a pearl and bead. Do not trim the excess 24-gauge wire. Bend the extending wire at about 1¾" (4cm) to begin the creation of a hook. Wrap the end around the coil, and trim the excess if necessary.

{2} WRAP HOOK IN FINER-GAUGE WIRE

Coil the remaining 24-gauge wire around the hook, creating a figure eight with each wrap. Wrap it around one side of the hook and then around the other side.

{3} FOLD WOVEN PORTION OVER FOR HOOK

Weave the wire back and forth through the hook until you reach the end, and then wrap the wire at the top of the hook to finish. Use pliers to create a crook in the end of the hook.

{4} ADD CROOK AT HOOK'S END

Bend the end of the hook up slightly. Dip all copper-wire orb pieces in liver of sulphur to blacken.

Green Victorian Dream
Ruth Rae, Crystal Neubauer, Liz Smith & **Dawn Supina**

Ruth used some commercial gold chains as the base for this green dream. In addition to Crystal's green button pendant, Ruth used several vintage buttons along with gemstones, crystals and bits cut from an old doily. Also included in the party are beautiful charms by Liz Smith and Dawn Supina.

Pillow Person
Katie Kendrick, Ruth Rae & **Kelly Snelling**

Katie Kendrick creates wonderfully whimsical characters in her paintings and fabric art. Here is a little pillow person she made to be worn as a pendant. When I saw it, I immediately started imagining a story of the little person's life. I was sure that she played a tiny horn, had a black cat and dreamed of flying like a bird in the night sky. So I painted these images onto small wooden disks to tell her tale. And clever Ruth brought them all together in this glorious piece.

Little Love
Sara Lechner, Martha Brown & **Ruth Rae**

Sara is a fiber artist whose work purely blows my mind. She works with textiles to create sculptural pieces that are so deeply layered, embroidered and embellished that you cannot begin to imagine how she accomplished it all. For this piece she made one of her famous characters into a small fabric pendant. Ruth took the little woman and made a necklace for her from love knots (see *Coiled-Wire Knots*, page 113), pearl circles and a soft fabric charm from Martha.

Nature's Gift

Ruth Rae, Shari Beaubien & Deryn Mentock

MATERIALS

19-gauge steel wire

22-gauge wire

24-gauge wire

basic jewelry tools (see page 8)

steel bench block

sandpaper

drill

.062 piano wire or 1/16"
   (2mm) mandrel

assorted fibers

assorted beads

seed beads

6mm beads, 3

Shari Beaubien frequently uses heart images in her magical mixed-media pieces. For this pendant, she brought out the shape of the heart in this little nutshell.

Using steel, Ruth created a necklace of long coiled links and sparkling beaded segments. Then, to show off the pendant, she created a wire-wrapped bar of fibers and beautiful beads, which is reminiscent of a cocoon. Lastly, she added a wonderful bird's nest, also made from steel, by Deryn. And there you have this gorgeous necklace known as Nature's Gift. This is surely a gift every girl would be overjoyed to receive.

Coil Links

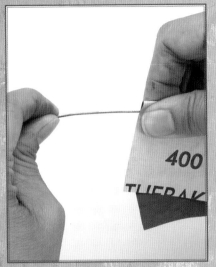

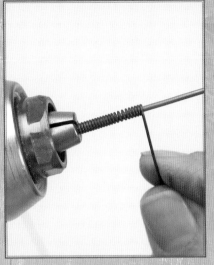

{1} POLISH WIRE

Clean a 24" (61cm) length of 19-gauge wire, and give it several passes with sandpaper or steel wool to polish it a bit.

{2} CREATE COIL

Cut a 24" (61cm) piece of 22-gauge wire and clean it in the same way. Insert it into a drill, along with a ¹⁄₁₆" (2mm) mandrel or piano wire. Coil the wire around the mandrel for about ½" (13mm).

{3} OVERLAP COILING

As the drill continues to rotate, pull the wire back toward the direction of the drill a bit to make it coil back on itself.

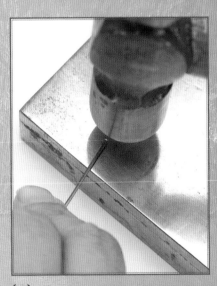

{4} REPEAT COILING PROCESS

Loosely coil the wire back to the end and start another ½" (13mm) coil. Repeat until you have at least seven sections.

{5} CUT COIL INTO SECTIONS

Cut the segments apart to make seven individual links.

{6} HAMMER ONE END OF WIRE

Cut a 3" (8cm) length of 19-gauge wire and hammer one end of it.

Fiber Bale

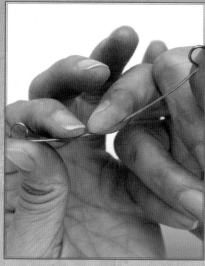

{7} CREATE HOOKED LINK

Slide a coil link onto the hammered wire and hammer the other end. Using round-nose pliers, coil the hammered ends in opposite directions. Repeat to make a total of seven.

{1} ARC WIRE FOR BALE

Cut a 4½" (11cm) length of 19-gauge wire, and use round-nose pliers to make a large loop at each end. Curve the piece slightly.

{2} WRAP WIRE IN FIBERS

Cut 11" (28cm) of assorted fibers and tie them to one end of the wire. Wrap the fibers around the wire several times.

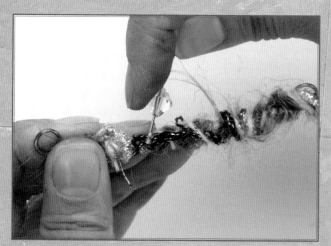

{3} ADD BEADS TO BALE

Cut a 24" (61cm) piece of 22-gauge wire and clean it with sandpaper. Attach the wire to one end of the fiber-wrapped armature, and start threading on seed beads and larger assorted beads. Start wrapping them around the piece. Continue wrapping and adding beads until the armature is covered.

{4} ASSEMBLE CHAIN

Rosary-wrap eight freshwater pearls and alternate them with the seven coiled links to form two halves of the necklace. (Note: A clasp is made by leaving one of the coil links open a bit to form a hook, and the other end of necklace will be a rosary-wrapped pearl with a jump ring attached to the end of it.) Attach the armature to the two ends of the necklace.

Bird's-Nest Charm

{1} CREATE SPIRAL

To create a bird's-nest element, begin by cutting 24" (61cm) of 19-gauge steel wire, and clean it with sandpaper. Use round-nose pliers to create a ⅜" (10mm) spiral on one end.

{2} ADD BEADS FOR EGGS

Cut a 4" (10cm) piece of 24-gauge wire and thread three 6mm beads onto it to represent eggs. Bring the ends of the wire together to cluster the eggs, and then twist the wires together. Attach the wire to the base of the wire spiral. Wrap it about four times.

{3} FORM WIRE INTO NEST

Start coiling 19-gauge wire around the eggs to form the nest.

{4} CREATE HANGER

When there's about 5" (13cm) of wire left, use the round-nose pliers to create a loop in the wire to use as a hanger.

{5} ATTACH NEST TO ARMATURE

Wrap the remaining wire around the nest to finish. Attach the nest to the armature with a jump ring.

FOREST FLOOR

Judy Scott, Martha Brown, Ruth Rae & Kelly Snelling

MATERIALS

24-gauge wire

basic jewelry tools (see page 8)

scissors

beading thread

beading needle

regular thread

stone chips

toggle bead

6mm beads

large stone beads

crimp beads

assorted decorative fibers

Oh, how we wish you could wear this necklace! It is earthy, weighty and looks as though it were cut down from the highest peak of a magical tree. You really do need to make yourself one of these.

When Judy Scott sent in these leaves, Ruth and I were jolted with excitement. They are so delicate, intriguing and flat-out pretty. We couldn't wait to design a piece around them. For an entire afternoon we pulled out stones and played with the colors, shapes and textures of what would best accompany these gorgeous centerpieces. We wanted to be sure to show them off and not to challenge them with our additions.

Ruth had a stash of gumball-sized garnets that set my head to spinning. They were combined with golden stick pearls and other chunky, faceted gemstones to create this glorious necklace known as Forest Floor. Martha Brown had made a special tree charm from a piece of wood, which we added to the main pendant so it could be worn on either side. After we selected the fruits for the leaves, Ruth worked like a little elf deep into the night on this intricate design. She couldn't sleep until she saw its completion. She swears it isn't nearly as difficult to make as it looks. Be patient, and your labors will reward you with a one-of-a-kind showstopper.

Free-Form Beading

{1} CREATE BEADED CIRCLE

Cut a 10" (25cm) length of 24-gauge wire. Thread on about 2" (5cm) of stone chips (garnet chips) and form them into a circle. Join the two ends by wrapping the shorter end around the long piece.

{2} WRAP WIRE EYE

Make an eye just outside of the beaded circle and, after wrapping it to secure it, coil the wire around itself for the entire perimeter of the eye.

{3} SECURE WIRE TO TOGGLE

Cut a 6" (15cm) piece of 24-gauge wire, and make a wire-wrapped eye at one end. Thread a bead—that can act as a toggle to the beaded circle—onto the wire and wrap the wire around the bead. Thread on eight seed beads and wrap the wire around the toggle bead a couple more times. Thread a piece of coated wire (the length you want the necklace) through the eye on the toggle and crimp the end with a crimp bead.

{4} SECURE STRAND TO CIRCLE

Thread beads onto the entire length of the wire, alternating three small beads with one large bead. At the end, secure the beaded circle to the length of wire using a crimp bead, leaving about ½" (13mm) of space between the beads and the circle.

{5} START FREE-FORM BEADING

Cut about 4' (1m) of beading thread and tie one end onto the beaded circle. Begin stringing a variety of beads onto the thread and trailing in and out of each of the beads already on the coated wire. This is a very organic process and will vary project to project, depending on the beads used.

{6} SECURE BEADING THREAD

Continue beading until you have completed the strand. Elements may be added with jump rings, if you like. To finish off the edges, you can tie fiber around the ends of the necklace to cover up the tied knots. I like to tie several knots around it before cutting it off.

Veiled Gothic Memories

Kelly Snelling & Crystal Neubauer

MATERIALS

28-gauge wire	laser photocopied
3/8" (10mm) dowel	images
basic jewelry tools	vintage letterpress
(see page 8)	block
paintbrush	mica
scissors	small tacks
awl	eye pin
drill and 1/16"	tulle
(2mm) bit	large beads
gel medium	vintage buttons
dimensional	burnt umber glaze
adhesive	
epoxy	

Crystal Neubauer made this utterly fantastic pendant from an old tintype photograph and a wooden letterpress block. Ruth and I ogled it long and hard trying to come up with just the right piece for it. Both of us wanted a chance to work it into our own piece. But one day Ruth left the studio to make us some lunch. That was all the time I needed to start wrapping beads in vintage netting and tulle. I swiftly rattled through Ruth's old buttons and pulled out a few small black ones and one big overcoat one to add to the twisted wire chain I was quickly concocting. By the time Ruth came back carrying a tray of lettuce wraps, I had claimed Crystal's pendant and given it a home in this Veiled Gothic Memories necklace. Much to my delight, Ruth thought it was grand, and we hope you do, too.

In case you don't have access to tintype photos, we are offering an example here using the same wooden block but with laser copies of your old photos underneath mica. This will give you a similar look without the tintypes.

Type Block Pendant

{1} TINT PHOTOS

Start with a two laser photocopies of a vintage photograph and apply burnt umber glaze to antique them.

{2} ADHERE PHOTOS TO BLOCK

Adhere one tinted copy to two opposite sides of a wood letterpress block, using gel medium.

{3} TRIM PIECES OF MICA

Trim pieces of mica to the same sizes as the two sides of the block the photos are on.

{4} ADHERE MICA TO PHOTOS

Adhere the mica over the photos with a small amount of dimensional adhesive. (A couple of drops are typically all that you need.)

{5} MAKE PILOT HOLES
Use an awl to make a small pilot hole in the center top and bottom of both mica pieces.

{6} HAMMER IN NAILS
Hammer small nails at the pilot holes.

{7} INSERT EYE PIN
Drill a ¹⁄₁₆" (2mm) shallow hole into the bottom of the block, and glue in an eye pin, using a bit of epoxy.

Tulle-Wrapped Bead

{1} WRAP TULLE AROUND BEAD
To make the tulle-wrapped beads, start with a large bead. Tear off a piece of tulle and wrap it around the bead, bringing the ends together.

{2} THREAD BEAD WITH WIRE
Trim a piece of 28-gauge wire to about 12" (30cm) and, while holding the tulle around the bead, thread the wire through the bead. Bring one end of the wire up and around the bead and back through the opposite hole.

Button Link

{3} CREATE EYES ON BEAD ENDS

Repeat for the other side of the wire and alternate wires and placement a few more times. Then create a wrapped eye at either end. Repeat for five more beads, randomly changing the placement of the wire.

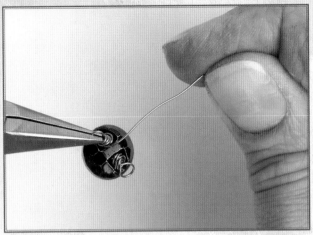

{1} ADD WRAPPED WIRE THROUGH HOLE

To use a faceted-button as a link, cut a 4" (10cm) piece of 28-gauge wire and give the button a rosary wrap (see page 110). Wrap the wire more times than usual to fill in the area between the button's hole and the edge of the button.

Free-Form Wire Links

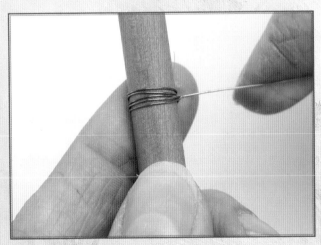

{1} WRAP WIRE AROUND DOWEL

Working directly off of the spool, wrap 28-gauge wire around a ⅜" (10mm) dowel five times.

{2} SECURE COIL WITH WIRE

Trim the wire to leave about a 4" (10cm) tail, and remove the coil from the dowel. Wrap the tail around the group of wires a few times and trim. Then, using what was trimmed off, wrap the group together on the opposite side. Repeat to make a total of eleven coil links.

Sweet Refuge

Joanna Pierotti, Judy Scott, Ruth Rae & Kelly Snelling

MATERIALS

14-gauge copper wire

24-gauge copper wire

basic jewelry tools (see page 8)

steel bench block

small piece of fiber art

During the process of working on this book, I had a crash course in jewelry making. Ruth is a fantastic teacher. She is very patient and knows how to start at the beginning and see the project through to the end. I work much more organically, which is a polite way of saying I make big piles of everything and am in constant motion, willing to try anything. Instead of having a big plan, I imagine the ending as the piece is occurring. This necklace is no exception.

I had an idea to build a copper frame and then attach Judy's beautiful nest with coordinating fibers onto it. I pounded and twisted the frame, made the long links, added beads and finally added Joanna's egg charm to the bottom. Then I took the whole thing to Ruth and asked her to boost it with her talents. We wanted to get as many hands on each piece as we could. But Ruth wanted me to discuss my process with her. She wanted to know why I had made the choices I had in my design. Process? Her entire question was longer than my process. She told me it makes much more sense to build the frame specifically for the piece I had in mind rather then to attempt to make the piece fit the frame. Ahhh. Years of experience really do teach you something. So she reworked the frame to fit Judy's piece, and together we created this Sweet Refuge.

Wire-Frame Pendant

{1} HAMMER COILED WIRE

Cut a 2¾" (7cm) length of 14-gauge copper wire. Create a small spiral on one end. Then hammer the coil and the rest of the length with a hammer.

{2} ADD TEXTURE

Hammer the end to splay it out a bit, and then add some texture with a cross-peen hammer.

{3} CREATE SPIRAL LINKS

Using round-nose pliers, roll the straight end in to create a bail.

{4} SHAPE WIRE INTO FRAME

Repeat to make another spiral link. Create four links from 14-gauge copper wire that are hammered and rolled at both ends (not spiraled). To create a frame for a piece of fiber art, start with a piece of 14-gauge wire, about 12" (30cm) in length, and shape it into a frame that leaves about ¼" (6mm) of space around the fiber piece. The wire should be long enough to overlap at the top.

{5} SECURE FRAME TOGETHER

If your fiber piece has a bale on it, thread it onto the frame. Then use 24-gauge copper wire to secure the two frame ends together by wrapping it.

{6} STRETCH PIECE TO FRAME

Cut a new length of 24-gauge wire and use it to sew the fiber piece to the frame all the way around in a whipstitch fashion. The finished pendant can be attached with a jump ring.

I get my love of painting from my mother, who is a very talented oil painter. And I have quickly gotten her hooked on jewelry making. We decided to have an exchange for this book. So we each took small wooden rectangles we purchased at the craft store and used them as our canvases to create pendants. My mom painted a colorful bird, and I painted the green and blue portrait of a girl. Then we had a terrific time twisting wire, making bead segments and using these special long glass beads for our pretty necklaces.

Mother–Daughter Collaborative Swap

Betty Whitlow & **Kelly Snelling**

Joanna took an old dog tag, wire-wrapped it and added a feminine touch with a pink flower and metal leaf. Ruth used this as the starting point for her necklace of vintage chain, metal lace, garnets and peach coin pearls. Lastly, she added a starfish and crystal charm that Holly made.

Metal Lace
Ruth Rae, Joanna Pierotti & Holly Stinnett

Joanna used ribbon and thread to sew up window screen into a little sack home for a bird egg. Ruth created a braided ribbon and seed bead necklace to accompany it. Lastly, she added this pretty etched copper and brass charm made by Cece.

Traveling Nest
Ruth Rae, Cece Grimes & Joanna Pierotti

Love Knot Necklace

Ruth Rae, Nancy Nelson, Martha Brown & Kelly Snelling

MATERIALS

19-gauge steel wire	burnt umber glaze
22-gauge steel wire	gel medium
drill	block beads, 3
¼" (6mm) mandrel	crystal beads, 2
piano wire or ¹⁄₁₆"	8mm bead
(2mm) mandrel	metal angel shape
basic jewelry tools	old book text or
(see page 8)	other paper
steel bench block	acrylic paint
jeweler's saw	pencil
bench pin	permanent marker
#13 knitting needle	
paintbrushes, one	
detail brush	

For this dreamy necklace, we began with one of Nancy's winged metal people. She had given this pendant butterfly wings and ballet slippers and added a dream to her heart. Martha had taken plain wooden block beads purchased at her local craft store and stamped them with blackbirds for a dramatic effect. Ruth took these elements and designed a gorgeous necklace out of heavy-gauge steel purchased at our local hardware store. She made many lovely links such as love knots, twisted jump rings and figure eights. My contribution was to saw all those twisted steel jump rings, a job not for the faint of heart.

Twisted-Coil/Cube Link

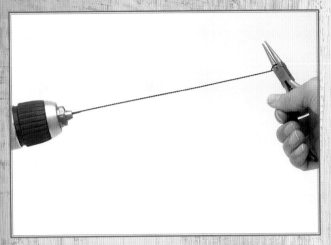

{1} TWIST LENGTH OF WIRE

Cut approximately 72" (2m) of 22-gauge wire and fold the length in half. Secure the two wire ends into a drill. Hold the folded end with round-nose pliers and turn the drill on (slow speed) to twist the wire.

{2} COIL TWISTED WIRE

Continue twisting until it is the tightness you want it. (The tighter the twisting, the harder it will be to work with.) Then secure the twisted wire and the piano wire into the drill. Turn the drill on (slow speed) and hold on to the twisted wire to coil it around the piano wire.

{3} CUT APART SECTIONS

Remove the coil from the mandrel. Cut the coil into ⅜" (10mm) sections.

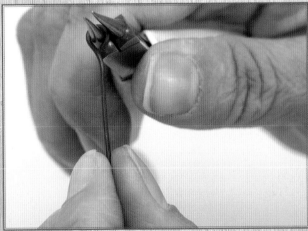

{4} MAKE LOOP

Trim a piece of 19-gauge wire to approximately 2" (5cm). With round-nose pliers, make a loop on one end.

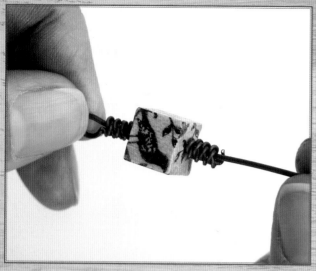

{5} THREAD ON COILS AND BEAD

Thread on one coil segment, a block bead, and then another coil.

{6} ADD LOOP AT OTHER END

Finally, make a second loop at the other end of the wire to complete the segment. Repeat two more times to make three segments. Also create two segments, with crystal beads instead of blocks, in the same manner.

Basic Rosary-Wrapped Bead

{1} MAKE FIRST EYE LOOP

Cut a 2" (5cm) length of 19-gauge wire and make a small loop at about ¾" (19mm) from one end. Hold the loop with pliers and wrap the excess around the base about one and a half times.

{2} ADD BEAD AND SECOND EYE LOOP

Trim any excess wire from the wrap. Thread on a bead and make another loop on the other side of the bead. Wrap the excess around and trim in the same manner as the first loop.

Arc & Bead Link

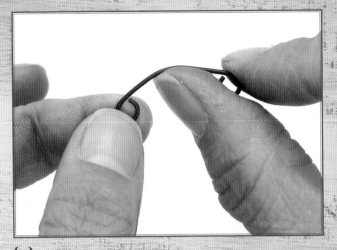

{1} CURVE LOOPED WIRE
Cut a 2" (5cm) length of wire and make an eye loop at each end. Curve the piece slightly.

{2} HAMMER WIRE
Hammer the entire piece to flatten it.

{3} OPEN UP ONE EYE
Using pliers, open up one eye a bit.

{4} ADD WRAPPED BEAD
Thread on a rosary-wrapped bead and then open the other eye a bit to thread on the other end of the wrapped bead.

S-Link

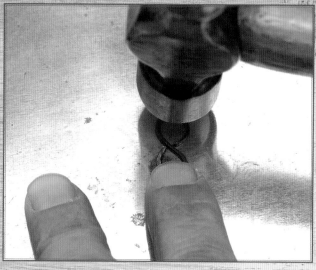

{1} CURVE WIRE IN OPPOSITE DIRECTIONS

Cut a 1¾" (4cm) piece of 19-gauge wire and create a large loop on one end. Curl the opposite end in the opposite direction to create a figure eight or S shape.

{2} HAMMER WIRE

Hammer the shape to flatten it.

Twisted-Wire Jump Rings

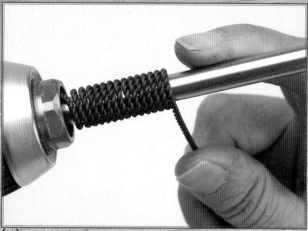

{1} CREATE TWISTED-WIRE COIL

To create twisted-wire jump rings, twist approximately 72" (2m) of 19-gauge wire using a drill, as you did on page 109. This time, coil the twisted wire around a ¼" (6mm) mandrel.

{2} SAW RINGS APART

Hold the coil, and cut the rings apart with a jeweler's saw.

Coiled-Wire Knots

{1} COIL WIRE AROUND NEEDLE

Coil a new approximately 72" (2m) length of 19-gauge wire around a #13 knitting needle.

{2} COUNT NUMBER OF RINGS

From one end of the coil, count four rings and pull it apart slightly.

{3} CUT SECTION APART

Cut the coil section apart.

{4} THREAD ONE SECTION ONTO ANOTHER

Cut two more sections. Pull one section apart slightly and link two coils together by threading one through the whole of the second.

MISSING LINK

Regular jump rings are created in the same manner as the Twisted-Wire Jump Rings; instead of coiling twisted wire around a mandrel, you begin with a single strand of wire and wrap that around your desired size of mandrel. Then cut the rings apart using either a saw or flush cutters.

{5} CONTINUE COILING
Continue coiling until the two coils are completely linked together.

{6} THREAD ON THIRD COIL
Lightly pull apart the third coil and link it simultaneously through the center of the first two coils to create a knot.

{7} ADD EYE SECTION
Cut a 2" (5cm) piece of 19-gauge wire and make an eye on one end with round-nose pliers. Thread on the knot, and then make a second eye on the other end.

Twisted-Wire Clasp

{1} WRAP TWISTED WIRE
To create the clasp, cut an 8" (20cm) length of 19-gauge twisted wire. Make a fold in it about 2" (5cm) from one end. Wrap the final 1" (3cm) of wire around the long section of wire.

{2} BEND HOOK SHAPE
Fold the end of the wire down for the hook, and then bend the end back slightly.

{3} CREATE EYE TO FINISH
Create two coils at the base of the wrapped portion, and then wrap the remaining wire around itself a final time to finish. Trim the excess wire.

Collaged-Angel Pendant

{1} TRACE WING SHAPES

For the pendant on this necklace, we use a metal angel shape as the base. For the wings, you can either paint the metal, or you can cover them with paper. If you want to cover them with paper, trace the general shape on the paper of your choice.

{2} PAINT DETAILS ON WINGS

Fold the paper in half, and cut out the wing shapes to create four wings. Apply a burnt umber glaze over the surface of the paper wings. Then, with a smaller detail brush, add details such as flower shapes. You could also collage images here.

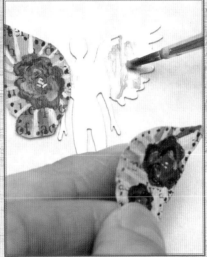

{3} ADD FINISHING TOUCHES

Continue painting until you are happy with your wings.

{4} ADHERE WINGS TO METAL

Use gel medium to adhere the painted wings to the metal shape.

{5} ADD TEXT

Add final details with a permanent marker, and add a word of text, if you like.

Fan Dance

Ruth Rae & Nancy Nelson

MATERIALS

18-gauge wire

24-gauge wire

12" (30cm) premade vintage
    chain

basic jewelry tools (see page 8)

6mm crystals and beads,
    assorted sizes

Nancy Nelson lives in Reno, Nevada, where she and her
husband make decorative fronts for slot machines. But clever
Nancy also uses the die-cut machines to create beautiful
winged metal pendants. Nancy turned this one into a gorgeous
geisha, which inspired Ruth to create this beautiful beaded
bar necklace known as Fan Dance.

Beaded Bale

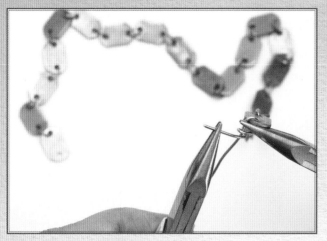

{1} WRAP ONE END OF CHAIN

This necklace uses 12" (30cm) of commercial vintage chain. Cut 5" (13cm) of 18-gauge wire and straighten it out. Cut 12" (30cm) of 24-gauge wire as well. Create an eye loop on the end of the 18-gauge wire, and wrap it onto one end of the commercial chain.

{2} BEGIN ADDING BEADS

Wrap the end of the 24-gauge wire onto the wrap of the 18-gauge wire, and thread on one 6mm bead. Wrap the 24-gauge wire around the 18-gauge wire and thread on another bead opposite the first. Then wrap the wire again.

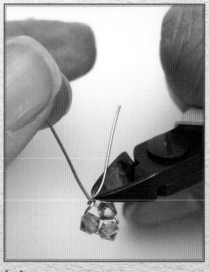

{3} ADD CRYSTAL BEADS

Continue alternating sides until you reach the end of the wire. Then begin going back down the beaded section and start threading on smaller crystal beads between the first set of beads, creating a checker pattern.

{4} CREATE BEAD DANGLES

When the second row of beads has been added, attach the other end of the 18-gauge wire to the opposite side of the chain. To create dangles to add to the chain, cut 4" (10cm) pieces of 24-gauge wire and thread on three crystal beads. For each, leave a 3" (8cm) tail, form a U shape and wrap the tail around the top.

{5} SECURE DANGLE TO CHAIN

Thread a 6mm bead onto the wire, and create a loop and link it onto the chain. Then wrap it to secure.

FLY

Shari Beaubien, Ruth Rae, Jennifer Rowland,
& Catherine Witherell

MATERIALS

20-gauge wire

clay blade

awl

T-pin

paintbrush

rubber stamp (for texture in clay)

gel medium

two-part resin (Envirotex)

clay sealer or clear nail polish

polymer clay

image

size-6 beading cord

clamshell crimps, 2

8mm pearls and crystals, assorted

leather cord

lobster clasp

Shari Beaubien created a bezel from polymer clay to showcase a tiny bird painting on this pendant. This is a really wonderful alternative to metal work (and it is easy and fast). If you're not a fan of soldering, this project is for you.

Shari's pendant inspired Ruth to adorn a necklace with leather, light green faceted crystal beads and fat freshwater pearls. Then she added a lovely precious-metal clay charm from Catherine and a dangling charm of found objects from Jennifer. All these elements come together in this sweet necklace that is reminiscent of spring.

Resin-Filled Clay Pendant

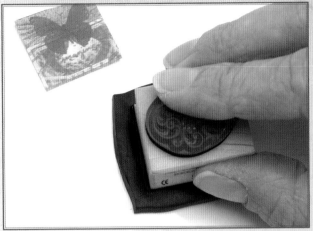

{1} PREPARE IMAGE AND CLAY

Condition and roll out enough clay to suit your chosen image. Set your image on the clay and trim it to leave a ¼" (6mm) border on all sides. To seal your image, use gel medium to coat the image on both sides and along the edges, and then set it aside.

{2} INDENT CLAY FOR IMAGE

To create a frame around the outside, push in the clay where the image will go. Use something square, such as the back of a stamp, to form the corners.

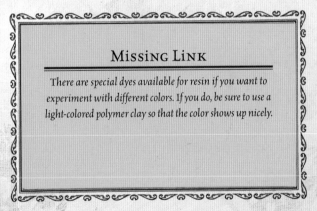

MISSING LINK

There are special dyes available for resin if you want to experiment with different colors. If you do, be sure to use a light-colored polymer clay so that the color shows up nicely.

{3} ADD TEXTURE TO CLAY

Stamp into the frame portion to give the clay some texture.

{4} ADD HOLES

Adhere the image to the frame with gel medium. Use an awl to make two holes at the top and one at the bottom.

{5} CREATE BEZEL LIP

Roll out into a thin rope a small amount of clay and add it around the perimeter of the image.

{6} POUR ON RESIN

Bake the piece according to manufacturer's directions and let cool. Mix up a small batch of resin (Envirotex) according to the package directions. Pour the resin over the surface of the image, filling but not overflowing the bezel section of the frame.

{7} SEAL CLAY

Babysit the piece for about fifteen minutes. If bubbles arise, they can be easily dislodged with the heat of a lighter. Then set the piece aside to cure. Give the remaining clay portion a coat of either clear nail polish or clay sealer.

Pearls & Leather Strand

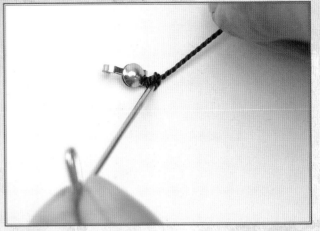

{1} KNOT CORD AND ADD CLAMSHELL

Knot the end of a long length of size-6 beading cord and thread it on a clamshell.

{2} TIE KNOT

Using a T-pin, tie a knot right next to the clamshell.

{3} ADD PEARLS AND ADDITIONAL KNOTS

Thread on the first 8mm pearl, and tie another knot. Thread on a second pearl and push it on tightly to tighten the knot.

{4} ADD LEATHER CORD

Continue adding knots and beads until the necklace is the length you want. Then crimp the other end of the thread to another clamshell. Secure one jump ring to each clamshell. Add additional elements such as the resin pendant or other dangles. Cut a length of leather cord to 13" (33cm) and fold it in half. Thread it through the ring of a lobster clasp. Wrap the cord with 20-gauge wire to secure it to the ring at the fold. Thread on one bead, and then wrap the cord together in the center. Thread on another bead, thread the ends through one jump ring on the strand of pearls and secure the ends with additional wire to finish.

I had been practicing making bead link segments with green freshwater pearls when we received Shari's Grow pendant. It has a lovely tree that she painted onto a big pinecone petal. Ruth took my pearls, Maija's stick bundles and Sally's seed dangles and put them all together to create this beautiful, nature-inspired necklace.

Grow

Ruth Rae, Kelly Snelling, Shari Beaubien, Maija Lepore *&* **Sally Turlington**

Songbird

Ruth Rae, Lelainia Lloyd *&* **Mija Marie**

Lelainia Lloyd created the songbird that is the centerpiece for this necklace. She used a tiny cog from her grandpa's workshop along with vintage sheet music, glitter, a little leaf and a cheery yellow bird. Ruth took the pendant and created a necklace of sparkling beaded clusters, to which she added Mija Marie's avant-garde charms. These are made from small glass fuses, transparent images of eggs, more sheet music and silver wire.

Ruth participated in a black-and-white-themed charm exchange led by Amber Dawn. Each artist created a black-and-white charm for every player. Ruth hung the group's amazing charms on a neat length of chain with rectangular twisted wire links to create this graphic charmer.

Black-and-White Charm Bracelet

Ruth Rae, Judith Thibaut, Amber Dawn Goldish, Catherine Witherell, Mija Marie, Martha Brown & Jessica Moreau-Berry

Resources

A Charming Exchange
www.acharmingexchange.com
Website for this book

ANDS Silver
www.andssilver.com
(323) 254-5250
Bali and Thai silver beads

Best Beads
www.bestbeads.etsy.com
unique gemstones

Cool Tools
www.cooltools.us
(888) 478-5060
dapping/doming blocks, liver of sulphur, precious metal clay

Dick Blick Art Materials
www.dickblick.com
(800) 828-4548
metal punch, liver of sulphur

Fire Mountain Gems & Beads
www.firemountaingems.com
(800) 355-2137
beads, findings, wire, metal clay, tools

Gem Faire & Bead Faire
www.gemfaire.com
fantastic West Coast (U.S.) traveling bead show

Glimmer Bead Trust
www.glimmerbeadtrust.etsy.com
luxury gemstones

Green Girl Studios
www.greengirlstudios.com
(828)298-2263
unique handcrafted beads, clasps, pendants

Harbor Freight
www.harborfreight.com
(800) 444-3353
alphabet/number metal stamping set

Invoke Arts
http://invokearts.com
(805) 541-5197
unusual rubber stamps

Jatayu—Connie Fox
www.jatayu.com
metal circle punch, tools, supplies, tutorials, inspiration

Just Simply Charming
www.justsimplycharming.blogspot.com
blog from our original charm swap

Manto Fev
www.mantofev.com
unusual vintage supplies

Metalliferous
www.metalliferous.com
metal, tools and supplies for jewelers and crafters

Otto Frei
www.ottofrei.com
jewelry tools and findings

Rio Grande
www.riogrande.com
(800) 545-6566
tools, findings, wire, beads

Silver Crow Creations
www.silvercrowcreations.com
(724) 379-4850
shrine supplies, art rubber stamps, vintage ephemera, unique beads

Thunderbird Supply Company
www.thunderbirdsupply.com
(800) 545-7968
sterling, copper and brass wire; beads; tools; findings

Tibetan Beads
http://tibetanbeads.com
chunky copal beads with sterling bead caps, pendants, antique beads

Tsukineko
www.tsukineko.com
(800) 769-6633
StazOn inkpads

Volcano Arts
www.volcanoarts.biz
metalsmithing tools and supplies, mica, gold leaf

Participating Artists

Shari Beaubien
{Canyon Country, California}
www.sharibeaubien.com
www.sharibeaubien.etsy.com

Martha Brown
{Toronto, Canada}
www.m-is-for-martha.blogspot.com
www.marthabrown.etsy.com

Dot Christian
{Frankston, Victoria, Australia}
www.dotslifeandart.blogspot.com

Debra Cooper
{Harlingen, Texas}
www.littleblackkitty.typepad.com
www.littleblackkittyart.etsy.com

Deborah Edwards
{Chicago, Illinois}
www.bellalunabeads.com
www.bellalunabeads.etsy.com

Lorraine George
{Round Rock, Texas}
www.evoke-designs.blogspot.com
www.lgeorge.blogspot.com

Marci Glenn
{Cornelius, Oregon}
www.picturetrail.com/mglenn

Amber Dawn Goldish
{New York, New York}
www.inventivesoul.blogspot.com
www.charms2007.blogspot.com

Cece Grimes
{Houston, Texas}
www.cecegrimes.etsy.com

Michael Johansson
{Robertsdale, Alabama}
www.polymerclayweb.com
www.mossyowls.blogspot.com

Katie Kendrick
{Belfair, Washington}
www.katiekendrick.com
www.joyouslybecoming.typepad.com

Sara Lechner
{Mank, Niederösterreich, Austria}
www.sibarita.etsy.com
www.thefabricofmeditation.blogspot.com

Maija Lepore
{Phoenix, Arizona}
www.maigirlz.typepad.com

Lelainia Lloyd
{Coquitlam, B.C., Canada}
www.tattered-edge.com
www.tatterededge.etsy.com

Mija Marie
{Eugene, Oregon}
www.picturetrail.com/loosemuse
www.loosemuse.etsy.com

Lou McCulloch
{Medina, Ohio}
www.metamorphosis.typepad.com/
metamorphosis
www.cafepress.com/glimpses

Trudy McLauchlan
{Foster, Victoria, Australia}
www.picturetrail.com/playingintheattic

Deryn Mentock
{Cypress, Texas}
www.mocknet.etsy.com
www.somethingsublime.typepad.com

Jessica Moreau-Berry
{Whitefield, Maine}
www.junquerevival.com
www.sweetpeas.motime.com

Fiona Mortimore
{Queensland, Australia}
www.thedecoratedsurface.wordpress.com
www.picturetrail.com/fionam

Nancy Nelson
{Reno, Nevada}
www.nancynelsonartstudio.com
www.nancynelson.blogspot.com

Crystal Neubauer
{Grayslake, Illinois}
www.otherpeoplesflowers.blogspot.com
www.otherpeoplesflowers.etsy.com

Jade Pegler
{New South Wales, Australia}
www.jadepegler.net
www.spectrescope.blogspot.com

Joanna Pierotti
{Volcano, California}
www.mosshillstudio.com
www.mosshill.blogs.com

Ruth Rae
{Claremont, California}
www.ruthrae.com
www.ruthrae.blogspot.com
www.ruthrae.etsy.com

Jennifer Rowland
{Austin, Texas}
www.jrowsjunque.blogspot.com

Judy Scott
{Kinross, Scotland}
www.judyscott.etsy.com
www.judy-scott.blogspot.com

Liz Smith
{Cleator, Cumbria, UK}
www.lizsmith.typepad.com/alterations

Kelly Snelling
{Irvine, California}
www.soulhumming.typepad.com
www.kellysnelling.etsy.com

Holly Stinnett
{Venice, California}
www.hollylovesart.blogspot.com
www.bichon4us.etsy.com

Dawn Supina
{Edmonton, Alberta, Canada}
www.dawnsupina.blogspot.com
www.picturetrail.com/canada_eh

Judith Thibaut
{Santa Fe, New Mexico}
www.judiththibaut.com
www.studiojudith.blogspot.com

Edina Tien
{Del Mar, California}
www.edinatien.blogspot.com

Sally Turlington
{Huntsville, Texas}
www.sallyt.typepad.com
www.sallyt.etsy.com

Kathy Wasilewski
{Midlothian, Virginia}
www.alteredantiquity.com
www.alteredantiquity.typepad.com

Betty Whitlow
{Mayfield, Kentucky}

Catherine Witherell
{Orinda, California}
www.happydayart.typepad.com
www.happydayart.etsy.com

Index

ABOUT THE AUTHORS

Ruth Rae's artistic path has traveled through photography, web design, fiber arts, decorative painting, polymer clay and metal clay. She made her first lost wax casting piece in a high school art class, but it wasn't until the 1990s that she discovered her love for cold-connection jewelry. She lives in California with her husband, two teenage children and their wild little dogs. She enjoys teaching and sharing her love of jewelry making and art with others.

Kelly Snelling is a Southern girl transplanted to California. She is a self-taught artist who believes she can do anything she sets her mind to. Her art and words have been published in several magazines and books. When she isn't playing tag with her dog and two little boys or dancing with her adorable husband, she can be found daydreaming, painting, singing, laughing, making BIG necklaces and living life loudly with every fiber of her soul.

INDULGE YOUR CREATIVE SIDE
WITH THESE OTHER F+W PUBLICATIONS TITLES

Semiprecious Salvage
Stephanie Lee

Create clever and creative jewelry that tells a story of where it's been, as metal, wire and beads are joined with found objects, some familiar and some unexpected. You'll learn the ins and outs of cold connections, soldering, aging, using plaster, resins and more, all in the spirit of a traveling expedition.

ISBN-10: 1-60061-019-6. ISBN-13: 978-1-60061-019-6
PAPERBACK, 128 PAGES, Z1281

PlexiClass
Tonia Davenport

Discover a modern, industrial twist on mixed-media art jewelry. *PlexiClass* features 30 cutting-edge projects that all start with plastic such as Plexiglas, vinyl or shrink plastic. In addition to learning how to cut Plexiglas, you'll also learn how to shape it into earrings, charms and pendants, and you'll see how easy it is to combine plastic with your favorite papers, embellishments and other mixed-media materials.

ISBN-10: 1-60061-061-7, ISBN-13: 978-1-60061-061-5
PAPERBACK, 128 PAGES, Z1753

Bent, Bound & Stitched
Giuseppina Cirincione

Collage, cards and jewelry with a twist! More than just beautiful step-by-step projects, there are techniques in this book that any aspiring artist will love. Among them are bending and shaping wire into letters and numbers, using a sewing wheel and acrylic paint to add texture to papers, making hinges from a portion of a rubber stamp, adding texture to cards with basic sewing, combining different gauges of wire to create different looks for jewelry, combining rivets and shrink plastic, using a basic silkscreen process along with collage, and reworking found objects into jewelry. *Bent, Bound & Stitched* is one piece of eye candy you will want to pull off your shelf time and time again.

ISBN-10: 1-60061-060-9, ISBN-13: 978-1-60061-060-8
PAPERBACK, 128 PAGES, Z1752

Pretty Little Things
Sally Jean Alexander

Learn how to use vintage ephemera, found objects, old photographs and scavenged text to make playful, pretty little things, including charms, vials, miniature shrines, reliquary boxes and much more. Sally Jean's easy and accessible soldering techniques for capturing collages within glass make for whimsical projects, and her all-around magical style makes this charming book a crafter's fairytale.

ISBN-10: 1-58180-842-9, ISBN-13: 978-1-58180-842-1
PAPERBACK, 128 PAGES, Z0012

These books and other fine North Light titles are available at your local craft retailer, bookstore or online supplier, or visit us at **www.mycraftivity.com**.